INTRODUCTION

"Man ist was er isst" is an old German saying which causes one to smile. The play on words simply means that one is what he eats. At the same time, the deeper meaning of this adage may well serve as an introduction to any critical analysis of a national culture. If Juan is indeed what he eats, we can assume also that a people's physical and geographic factors determine the course not only of each individual citizen's life but also of the national culture in which he exists.

Within the last 400 years, however, there has been an intellectual explosion in thinking about the nature of humankind in so far as its physical existence is concerned. There have been multiple explanations and theories espoused as to the wider aspects of man's journey on this planet.

Academic disciplines in all fields interpret mankind as having economic, social, psychological, religious, political, aesthetic, and philosophical components, all of which influence our lives on multiple levels and to various degrees. The integration of these multiple causations to our actions can be seen in both personal and cultural ways. The first is obvious and gives us a way to examine our own shortcomings. The second looks at man's eternal struggle to explain the purpose of life itself.

There is a continual gnawing intellectual curiosity as to why or how certain events happened, particularly those which caused significant changes in the course of international, national and individual existence. Natural disasters wreak havoc in our societies and disrupt existence, often fatally, and in large numbers. Yet, the truly great disasters of modern life have been caused by man, himself.

The first half of the twentieth century was delineated by two cata-
clysmic events, World War I and World War II. The harsh reality of
World War I is hard to overstate. The concert of Europe was wracked
from stem to stern in almost every aspect of human existence. Whether
one's nation was on the winning or losing side in the struggle did not
seem to make much difference in assessing the outcome. The seemingly
measured pace at which society had moved when the twentieth century
opened had given way to total warfare which involved noncombatants
and regular citizens of all ages. President Woodrow Wilson's prophecy
was that unless all the nations joined a League of Nations to keep the
peace, there would be another world war in 20 years. He was correct in
his prognostication, and the second war was worse in many ways. The
advent of vast air armadas in many countries brought the war right into
civilian homes on a level which was beyond our imaginations.

The greatest event in this author's life was World War II, and
more specifically the struggle between the Empire of Japan and the United States. It was my encounter with a Japanese prisoner of war, described
in Chapter 11, and his willingness to cooperate with my interrogation,
that made me want to explore the way that Japanese culture had trained
its soldiers and created their mindset. The Japanese armed forces were
constantly reminded that they were fighting for the emperor and that they
should die fighting rather than surrender or be captured. I was aware of
the Imperial Rescript written by General Yamagata, as detailed in Chapter 3, which had created a special relationship between Japanese military
forces and the Emperor. I cannot remember any operation in the entire
Pacific Theater of operations which did not involve banzai attacks near
the end of the battle or places where Japanese soldiers hid out in small
holes or caves waiting for our troops to go by so they could shoot one or
two before they took their own lives.

The more I thought about this, the more I became intrigued as
to what kind of a society could produce soldiers who would inform so
openly against their own nation. My search for answers extended far beyond World War II, both in time and scope. Realizing that war itself
brings out both the best and worst aspects of human behavior, I have
tried to resolve the varying views of that struggle by looking at the cultural

REFLECTIONS
ON THE PACIFIC WAR

A Marine interpreter remembers

by Dr. Noel L. Leathers

ISBN# 978-1481202275

Noel L. Leathers

CONTENTS

backgrounds of both Japan and the United States. I have arranged the book so that it begins with the settlement of the Japanese archipelago, covered briefly in Chapter 1, with limited descriptions of the physical characteristics and an examination of the very significant role they played and how they affected the social and political formulations which evolved over the centuries after the first settlers arrived.

I have sketched what led up to the attack on Pearl Harbor in Chapters 5 and 6 and the consequential course of the war that followed it in the following chapters, from the vantage point of my own participation in it. I then continued by reviewing these and subsequent events from the perspective of the twenty-first century. It ends with an exploration of modern Japan and some of my conclusions, in Chapter 13. I have tried to explain how a civilization of a nation could develop a modern culture incorporating such actions. It has been a worthwhile experience for me and hope it will for the reader.

I determined to write this book after attending a commemoration of the 65th anniversary of the Battle of Iwo Jima. It was well attended by the children of the men who served there, the Kids of Iwo Jima. Most of the men who came back from World War II didn't talk about their experiences, so it's only recently that their children are learning what happened there. As the former soldiers age, they begin to come to terms with their lives and to talk and write about this era. And the children are now learning about it.

It is to the Kids of Iwo Jima that I dedicate this book.
Dr. Noel L. Leathers

1

EARLY JAPANESE SETTLEMENT AND GROWTH

In order to understand the Japanese society and how it affected Japan's relations with the United States and the rest of the world, it is important to see how its culture developed in accordance with its history and geography.

Starting about 3000 years ago, migratory tribes began to arrive on the Japanese archipelago, coming from several areas. Some, from the mainland areas of Asia, settled primarily in the southern part of Japan. Others came from islands in the southwest Pacific, including Micronesia and Polynesia. Still others came from the Siberian area, and they were usually whiter in skin color and much larger. Descendents of these people are easily recognized by their size. The result of these migrations over several centuries was an integration of these peoples into a race which is known today as the Japanese.

According to its mythology, Japan was founded on a date equivalent to February 11, in 660 B.C., when the Sun Goddess descended from the clouds and placed her son, Jimmu Tenno, on the throne. It has been thought by Japanese historians and others that the line of emperors has been unbroken since that date. Therefore the current emperor, Emperor Akihito, is a deity and carries the spirit name of Heisei. His father, Hirohito, had the spirit name of Showa throughout his reign from 1926 to 1989.

The four main islands which constitute the mainland, Hokkaido, Honshu, Shikoku, and Kyushu, stretch in a necklace-like form from north to south, and they, plus the 200 or so smaller islands in the archipelago, lie approximately 500 hundred miles off the Asian continent. This distance protected the island kingdom from the great power of China for many centuries while simultaneously isolating its people from foreign influences.

Mountain chains run through most of the islands from north to south and divide the eastern and western areas of the nation in significant ways. The land stretching from this spine down to the sea is separated by ridges, creating independent valleys. This served for many centuries served to keep agricultural communities somewhat isolated from their neighbors. The arable land constituted only 14% of the total land and hence required intensive cultivation along the valley floors. It required constant efforts to wrest more precious hectares by terracing the mountain sides of the valleys to produce more food.

Even as late as the thirteenth century there were instances of communities disappearing through starvation though adjacent valleys had sufficient food supplies. The topography of the land simply prevented lateral transportation of any significant materials and resulted in periodic food shortage disasters. The planting of rice seedlings at the appropriate time of the season, harvesting and storing significant reserves were all vitally necessary for survival. This factor should not be overstressed but it did contribute to the unique social system which gradually evolved over countless centuries. Although the early settlers came from a wide geographic area, the importance of having enough food to survive produced very similar social arrangements among the villages even though the villagers were not in contact with others.

Fortunately, Japan was surrounded by water, and the fishing industry also became a major source not only of food but also of wealth. The irregular coastline provided many areas conducive to fishing, and later the shipping and fishing industries. Nearly all movement of food and goods was confined to coastal waters, which gradually transferred items to areas otherwise shut off by natural terrestrial barriers.

Japanese production of goods was usually confined to areas which were either on the coast or very close to the shore. As testament to the importance of shipping and fishing to the Japanese economy, the merchant marine had grown to more than 12 million tons of commercial shipping by the outbreak of World War II.

Given the lack of arable land and almost total lack of any mineral assets, it was essential that the production of food from planting to harvesting became the overriding fact of life in these villages. The absolute survival of the villagers depended on their cooperation to dig irrigation canals and trenches along the sides of the hills and plant the food in a unified communal effort. It also required that the maintenance of the canals and trenches carrying water to the fields had to be the total responsibility of the entire population. These fundamental facts of life in the villages led to the slow development of a socio-political system which emphasized the importance of the community acting together if it were to survive.

Councils evolved to make decisions concerning the use of water, the timing of planting and harvesting, and whatever else was necessary. This was shared by the group rather than through individual actions and decisions. Over the centuries, these village councils tended to be led by the older, more experienced, men of each village. Similarly, the range and scope of council authority grew as well. The decision process gradually became institutionalized and the councils gradually assumed authority in other areas of village life. Not everyone would or could agree with the decisions of the council, nor others whose social behavior became disruptive. Consequently, over time the council assumed the authority to expel miscreants from the village in the name of maintaining a peaceful society.

Thus groupism became ingrained into the very fiber of Japanese society. To be expelled from one's group was equivalent to being exiled and caused a shameful loss of face in addition to threatening one's survival.

In the third century A. D., more than 100 Chinese scholars came to study these people living off the coast of Asia on the Japanese islands. Their 20 years of observations became the so-called Wei Chronicles. They commented repeatedly on how orderly and how prone to obey the people were; even though they could not perceive any formal political structure of control.

This contact with China began a relationship which over several hundred years served to enrich and broaden Japanese society. During the seventh and eighth centuries, Chinese culture was all the rage in Japan, and Mother China customs were widely adopted. While the intensity of contact and Chinese popularity declined by the tenth century, it is difficult to over-estimate this era's great influence on Japanese thought and daily life.

Mother China taught her neighbors a wide variety of skills in making items such as paper, ceramics, and lacquer ware. Japanese artisans learned quickly and were adept at improving on the manufacture of these and other items. The Japanese also learned how to build cities based on the Chinese grid system, which they used to build their first capital, Nara.

More important, the Japanese decided to use the Chinese system of writing, with its individual characters, and then developed two phonetic systems of their own. Lady Murasaki's *Tales of Genji*, published in 1000 A.D. was the first book written in Japanese.

Even in this early period, the Japanese became aware that there were other nations on this earth which were decidedly more advanced and that they could profit greatly by borrowing and adapting much of their cultures to Japan's advantage. This is still a characteristic of modern Japan, manifested by their willingness to purchase foreign patents for their industries, which is faster and cheaper than sponsoring basic research.

From the Nara period in the eighth century through the sixteenth century, a semi-feudal system emerged, with a long line of almost power-less emperors or empresses who held court in Heian, which known as Kyoto today. From the descriptions of court activities we have, it seems that there was very little of any real significance to the nation that transpired. Many are the descriptions of poetry contests and social hours and teas, which were held on a regularly scheduled basis.

Daimyos and samurai

Since the national administration of the country did not exist in any mean-ingful sense, it was almost inevitable that local clan leaders, who successively controlled various geographical areas, would assume the authority to handle affairs in their own area. They ignored the Emperor's court, except when they pressured it for specific privileges like land grants requiring a royal sig-nature. These local daimyos ruled their domains with an iron hand and frequently conspired among themselves to gang up on a neighboring daimyo to seize his territory. These feudal struggles had created local jealousies and permitted continual pirating and interruption of trade on a major scale.

In many ways, this resembled the feudal structure which was evolving in Western Europe during the same centuries. The local chieftains continually sought to expand their influence through military strength but oftentimes also through intermarriages and agreements about economic privileges. Political history became one of the rise and fall of various groups, all of whom claimed legitimacy from the Imperial court. Though the leaders of these groups acted independently of the Emperor and succeeded in establishing themselves in various parts of the country as the dominant force, they paid lip service to the existing Imperial court and either sent him a large force of their samurai to occupy an area around the court, bringing pressure for the Imperial seal and signature to be applied to land titles.

The lack of centralized political power to maintain order and to subdue both piracy along the coasts and armed groups of highwaymen required that local chieftains be responsible for maintaining law and order in their area. Over the centuries, it had become necessary for the villagers to find some means of defending themselves from these raiding parties, which seized whatever was available and in some instances actually caused severe suffering because of food shortages among the villagers.

As time progressed, the villagers decided that it would be to their advantage to hire some form of protection against these raids. Well before the arrival of the Wei chroniclers from China in the third century, the councils of elders in the villages had negotiated some form of agreement with military aggregates to protect them from these pirate raids.

The specialization of the individuals involved in these protective organizations resulted in the development of a warrior class called samurai. These samurai became well trained in the use of swords and daggers and bows and arrows. As time passed, these samurai were assembled under the leadership of a particular family which functioned in a particular area to maintain law and order.

The struggles among the various samurai leaders and their followers were exceptionally brutal. Punishment was meted out by the various samurai in the villages under their watch. To a certain degree, they became a law unto themselves, and if villagers conducted themselves or did something to which they were opposed they simply cut off their heads.

When a group of families set out for another destination during this era, it was necessary that they have an armed guard to accompany them. They also had one more participant in the entourage, the Fortune Keeper. This unique person walked along 100 paces or so behind the others, and his job was to attract all the evil that might occur to those upfront and absorb all of the evil. He was an extremely dirty person, never took a bath, did not speak to women, wore old ragged clothes and behaved like a mourner. He would often perform outlandish dances, hopping and jumping around to attract the evil forces.

In contrast to the Fortune Keeper is the story of Yamato-dake, or Yamato the Brave. According to the story, Yamato left his home at 15 years of age and set out for Kyushu, where there was an evil chieftain. He disguised himself as a girl and gained access into the chieftain's castle and then stabbed him to death. He continued to fight barbarians and finally went to the Shrine at Ise, where his sister was the high priestess. She gave Yamato a great sword, which he called Kusanagi.

Upon leaving the Shrine he took a boat to cross the Inland Sea. A great storm came up, and great waves washed over his small boat. His mistress, Orange Blossom, sacrificed herself by jumping into the waters and thereby calming the storm so that Yamato could continue.

He sought out the barbarians with his great sword and eliminated many of them. He was now worn out and was attacked by wild beasts in the hills, but a great white dog, which Yamato thought to be deity, came and saved him. Shortly thereafter, totally exhausted, he slumped down on a lonely moor and suffered a solitary death. His body became a white deer, which ascended rapidly in to the sky. The Emperor, on hearing of Yamato's death, ordered that a monument be built at the spot where he died and went up to the skies in the form of a deity. This recognition by the Emperor was considered the greatest praise anyone could attain.

This kind of mythology was repeated over and over again to young children because it was not only exciting but emphasized the kind of character that their parents wanted their children to have. A young handsome man went forth to conquer evil, used disguises intelligently, worked for the good of society by destroying evil forces, and finally had a lonely death on a cold mountain and then rose into the sky.

The feudal or semi-feudal era continued for several hundred years, but then a group of leaders came together in the last third of the sixteenth century and united all the domains into a united nation.

2

THE SHOGUNATE

The consolidation of the feudal system was eventually accomplished, largely through the efforts of three military leaders in the last decade of the sixteenth and the first years of the seventeenth centuries.

Oda Nobunaga was the first of the triumvirate. Nobunaga was born in 1534 into a family where the father was a wealthy government official in the Owari province, one of the smaller areas in the central part of Honshu. For over 200 years prior to his birth, Japan had been rocked by internal struggles among samurai who were constantly seeking to increase their wealth by cooperating or teaming up with others so that they could overpower another one and seize control of that land. Names were changed, family lines crossed in order to gain better tactical advantage of a situation. Several families became predominant in this period and allegedly ruled their territories in the name of the Emperor. The Imperial residence was in Heian, also known as Kyoto, and the incumbent Emperor relied on influential families for his financial support.

The brutality of the period almost defies description, but if you were on the losing side, the winners would give you the opportunity of committing an honorable suicide or being beheaded as if you were a common criminal. The number of the samurai grew to nearly 450,000 individuals who gathered themselves into groups behind a leader and during the Middle Ages conducted often an internecine warfare.

Nobunaga was described as being a rather wild youth who paid very little attention to the responsibilities of his family. He was 17 years old when his father died, and so terrible was his behavior during the funeral services that one of his father's relatives committed suicide to indicate his total disgust. Because of this, he settled down and determined that he should expand the holdings of the family through any means possible. Over the next eight or nine years he managed to seize control of more than a dozen other domains after brutally putting those leaders to death or entering into an agreement with those who would become an ally. He gained control over several local daimyos and built an ever increasingly large army.

Nobunaga was extremely ambitious and had launched an invasion of the Korean peninsula, which although initially successful, had to be aborted just short of the northern border. The force, in excess of 200,000 troops, entered Korea from the south, and when his army passed through Pyongyang, the Chinese ruler sent a force in to protect Korea from being taken over by Japan. (This scenario was repeated in 1950).

Nobunaga constructed the largest castle in the entire nation close to Heian. His consecutive string of military victories over his opposition was unparalleled and made possible not only because of his strategic skills but his willingness to adopt new weaponry such as Portuguese muskets and archery tools that were in advance of anything else in the nation.

One of the younger leaders, who later became known as Tokugawa Ieyasu, had changed sides in one of the turf battles and joined Nobunaga's forces. He was the second of the triumvirate. The third was Toyotomi Hideyoshi, born into a peasant family in 1536 with rather monkey-like features that earned him the nickname Little Monkey. His parents lived on land that was under the control of General Nobunaga, and his parents wanted their son to attend school since he wasn't physically strong. In a short time, he ran away from the school and got a position as a servant in the house of Nobunaga, who immediately assigned him military duties. He participated in some small battles and established himself as an excellent military leader. As a consequence, after two or three victories Nobunaga promoted him in rank and shortly thereafter made him a samurai. This was a rare occurrence, but recognition of his extraordinary military record.

The official listing for the death of General Nobunaga is that he died by assassination. In reality, he was captured by an enemy samurai who had been tipped off by one of Nobunaga's aides. He was offered the choice of either committing suicide or of having his head chopped off as if he were a common criminal. He chose the former, but it's hard to call this an assassination. Prior to his death in June, 1582, Nobunaga had discussed at length with Hideyoshi and Tokugawa his plans to unify all of Japan under one rule. This resulted in a rather loosely held agreement among the three to cooperate. Their aim was to extend control both to the north from the feudal capital of Heian and simultaneously move westward towards Shimonoseki and southward to incorporate Kyushu and Shikoku. To accomplish their goals it would be necessary to overcome all resistance from all resistance from local daimyos.

After Nobunaga's death, Hideyoshi and Tokugawa agreed to coalesce their forces and continue their efforts to eliminate the feudal structure and to replace it with a national government, under a shogunate, with Tokugawa as shogun. They decided to move the capital from Heian to the mud flats where Tokyo is located today. This would not only signify a major break from the existing system but would give the shogun a new base of operations. They called the new capital Edo, and this name lasted for more than two and a half centuries. The significance of this decision to move the capital city was not readily apparent, but it provided a physical area where the power of the shogun could be exercised more swiftly and securely.

Reforms

Hideyoshi had been made kampaku, or chancellor, and at once issued reforms to stabilize Japanese society: Society would be divided into four hereditary groups, and each group had a specific area of responsibility. The first class was called the samurai, the warriors, whose duty it was to protect the nation from invasion or internal disruptions. Only samurai could carry arms. This simple step had an immediate impact on ending much internal strife.

The second class constituted the farming sector which was to produce food for the nation. The third class was made up of artisans, who made weapons, tools, ships and other items requiring a certain level of skill. Finally, the fourth group included traders, merchants and bankers who did not produce anything. There was no recognition of the fine arts and consequently the theater and stage areas evolved to meet the need of the upper classes. There were certain periods during the life of the Shogunate when the arts proved to be the most innovative aspect of the national culture.

Hideyoshi was a multi-talented individual and very interested in the artistic side of life. He popularized the very formal tea ceremony with elaborately designed utensils. He became a student of Noh dramas and actually performed from memory an astounding 10 of such plays. His influence on Japanese society at a very critical time was profound. Indeed, many Japanese have referred to him as being the George Washington of their nation.

Once the shogunate had established control over the four main islands, the distribution of land among the daimyos was determined. These separate sectors resembled a checkerboard, and in the selection and allocation the shogun was careful to separate the tozama lands, the lands belonging to daimyos not loyal to him, from each other so that they could not get together and plot opposition to his rule. The loyal daimyos were called the fudai.

The wealth of each area was measured in koku of rice, equal to five and one half bushels. If the daimyo had been fighting alongside the shogun's army, he would receive a grant of land with a higher rice production than those who had opposed the shogun's forces.

The shogunate also instituted the office of metsuke. These were auditors who traveled annually to each daimyo's domain to check on the rice production and at the same time kept their eyes and ears attuned for any sounds of budding opposition to the national government. They traveled in groups of three, since Tokugawa wanted to make sure that the metsuke would not conspire against him. He felt that if there were three it would be unlikely three would come to an agreement if the penalty for conspiring against the government was death.

Another part of the government's plan to keep the daimyos under control was the adoption of an Alternate Residence policy. It required the daimyos to spend every other year in Edo serving the Shogun's needs. The following year, when the daimyos returned to their domains, they had to leave their families in Edo to guarantee their good behavior.

This prompted a rapid construction of housing in the new capital city for families and servants and represented a severe strain on the financial resources of the daimyos, particularly the tozama ones.

The final step in making sure of the consolidation of power was the institution of a Seclusion Policy, which effectively closed the nation's borders to all foreigners. Tokugawa's grandson, Iemitsu, further refined this limitation on all foreign influences. There was only one small island in the harbor of Nagasaki in southwestern Kyushu where fewer than a dozen Dutch traders were permitted to stay. Their access to the city itself was severely limited.

The policy also stipulated that any foreigners who landed in Japan would be executed at worst and incarcerated at best. This effectively cut off nearly all contact with the western world at a time when great intellectual activity and new discoveries were taking place. Japanese scholars, for instance, thought the language of commerce was Dutch because of its small colony of Dutch traders. It was not until Commodore Matthew C. Perry's visit in the 1850s that they discovered they had learned the wrong language.

The policies of the shogunate were all announced and implemented in the name of the Emperor, who continued to exist as a remote figure with divine attributes. He had no authority but existed on the generosity of the current shogun. His existence and purpose became intertwined with the Shinto religion in the eyes of the populace. The mythology of the Sun Goddess as his ancestor and as the creator of the great natural beauty of the land was instrumental in the development of a sense of national identity of the populace.

Trade grows

The implementation of the shogun's policies not only eliminated piracy on the seas around the nation but also made it possible to travel on land with a sense of security heretofore unknown. Internal trade began to develop, and trading houses began to appear, with warehouses in ports along the coast. The production of some goods and tools made by the artisan class expanded to meet a growing internal market.

The Alternate Residence system also produced some unexpected results, since the mandatory year's stay in Edo left many daimyos with little to do except appear at formal occasions upon command of the shogun. It gave them time to discuss matters of concern among themselves about local problems in their home areas, including better rice growing techniques, new equipment, and improving financial opportunities. As a byproduct of their continual interaction, regional and local dialects of the language tended to disappear.

Since the daimyos' families had to remain in Edo, it was necessary to build living quarters for them and to establish schools where their children could learn. Consequently, areas of Edo became clearly identified as neighborhoods which needed housing, schools, new government buildings and entertainment centers, contributing to rapid growth in Edo and other coastal cities.

Tokugawa had created a national council of elders earlier to advise him on issues and found it very well received by the people who were very familiar with the old village councils of elders. As the population increased and the urban centers became ever larger, it became apparent that the council of elders as constituted was not equipped to handle problems of both a political and legal nature in what was becoming a more sophisticated society . Consequently, the national oversight of urban areas was delegated to a junior council of elders.

The tight financial control over the income of the daimyos, who were also faced with new costs for housing and schooling as well as required travel to Edo, created problems which were handled in a unique fashion by the ruling shogun. On three separate occasions during the tenure of the shogunate, the shogun would issue an edict simply wiping out the debts of the daimyo class regardless of the damage done to merchants, traders and suppliers of services of all kinds. The latter had no recourse but to obey the decrees and start over again.

One factor which enabled the merchants to sustain these setbacks was the steady increase of business activity. It is frequently overlooked, but the internal economy grew in size to meet the growing appetite of the people in an environment without any foreign competition. Estimates have varied, but the total population grew to nearly 30 million by the time of Perry's visit in the middle of the nineteenth century.

The Seclusion Policy had been strengthened by Tokugawa Iemitsu and rigorously enforced. By 1624, all the Spanish traders and missionaries had been driven out and the Portuguese by 1640. Trade with the Philippines was eliminated, and severe limitations placed on anyone wishing to go abroad. An uprising by Christians in Kyushu was mercilessly put down, killing over 37,000.

The 250 years of the Tokugawa shogunate created a situation in which the Japanese economy grew at a steady pace throughout the entire period. The absence of any competition from abroad and the establishment of internal peace provided an opportunity for the population not only to grow but also to enrich its existence with the advent of newer ways of doing things. Private schools began, at first only for the families of the daimyos but increasingly for other samurai.

The government oversaw the creation of a banking system, and for the first time Japan had a currency with some coins being issued by the government. Some of the biggest names in the Japanese economy had their origins during the early part of the 1700s.

The number of samurai increased to nearly 450,000, which stimulated a steady increase in the number of artisans who became experts in making swords and other weapons. This economic growth provided for the employment of many in the clothing industry which made it possible for some women to work in their homes and increase the family income. The steady growth of the population and of economic goods provided a solid basis for future generations long after the shogunate had become dim in our memories. The three leaders made great contributions to the growth of the nation and eliminated frequent feudal infighting which was holding the country back.

The early years of the eighteenth century were marked by the production of Japan's greatest play, *The 47 Ronin*, the last eruption of Mt. Fuji in 1703 and a growing restlessness among the daimyos. The drama of the *47 Ronin* emphasized many of the same virtues as first introduced into the national culture by the mythical hero, Yamato-dake, stressing the virtues of military service to the nation and recognition that death maybe the highest level of sacrifice .

The 47 Ronin drama as a highly involved plot and takes more than one night to perform. It is still the most significant stage production in modern Japan. Between 1997 and 2007 the drama had been performed yearly. A ronin is a samurai who does not have a leader or who has lost one. The drama revolves around the lives of these ronin after their leader was killed. They blame themselves for letting this happen and plot to avenge his death. They finally achieve their goal and ultimately take their own lives as expiation of their failure. Each production has a different interpretation of events and the denouement causes heated discussions as to which is more accurate. Since these issues deal with the core of the martial spirit and ethics the interpretations will continue for many years.

3

༺❀༻

Japan Opens Up

The visit to Japan by Commodore Matthew Perry in 1853 set off a series of events which ultimately led to the creation of modern Japan and the demise of the centralized feudal system that Tokugawa had established. Perry's entry into the bay and show of U.S. naval power set in motion forces far beyond anything the American government had anticipated.

The U.S. made demands to the ruling elite of Japan that the Seclusion Policy be ended and ports opened for commercial vessels trading in far eastern waters of the Pacific. Crews of these ships were not to be molested and provisions and fresh water were to be made available.

After some confusion, and in desperation about these new demands, the shogun leaders asked the daimyos for advice. This set off shock waves among these landed lords, since this was the first time in nearly 250 years that they had ever been asked for their opinion. Their response: to oppose giving in to foreign demands. Next, the shogunate asked the advisers to the Emperor what course of action to take. These officials also advised the shogun leadership to refuse the foreign demands. However, the fact that the shogunate sought advice was almost immediately interpreted as a sign of weakness.

The shogunate's confusion about what to do continued for several months without resolution, and when the Americans returned in the spring of 1854, the Bakufu, or government administration, agreed to sign the Treaty of Kanagawa–probably because it had no other choice.

From this time on, there was a gradual decrease in the ability and capacity of the Bakufu to carry out its responsibilities. The Imperial advisers saw in this an opportunity to reassert some of the Emperor's power, and steadily fanned the flames of unrest among the daimyos, who grew ever more antagonistic toward the existing Shogunate. The Treaty of Kanagawa in 1854 and subsequent treaties worked out by U.S. Ambassador Townsend Harris included provisions for extraterritoriality, which stipulated that if a foreign subject broke the law, he would be tried in his own nation's court system. The Japanese bitterly resented this clause which contributed to the steady decline of the authority of the government. It was also becoming apparent that the samurai class could no longer provide protection for the nation.

The transformation of the nation from an isolated, military-dominated country into the modern era continued apace for the next decade. By 1860, the shogun's government had signed similar treaties with other modern nations, and the establishment of foreign consulates and embassies was a constant source of resentment. The treatment of foreigners was frequently of a serious nature and led to the British bombardment of the port of Kagoshima in 1863 over this issue.

After an abortive attempt to overthrow the Bakufu, the leaders of the Choshu clan rose in revolt in their own domain and killed or exiled their own older military leaders. They seized control and armed their troops with new rifles in organized rifle companies, as did the Satsuma clan. A combination of intrigue by the advisors of the Emperor and the plotting of the Choshu and Satsuma clans caused the Shogunate armies to simply disperse when the newly equipped rebel armies approached the national capital.

This created the opportunity for the restoration of the Emperor as the symbolic head of the nation. This revolution was called the Meiji Restoration so as to put a better spin on the fact of actual revolution.

The new emperor was named Meiji, meaning the Enlightened Era. As he was only 16 years of age at the time, the fate of the nation lay rather in the hands of the Satsuma and Choshu clans, who had led the anti Shogunate movement. One major fact is that these young samurais had already ousted the older Choshu and Satsuma clan leadership, a pattern that repeats itself throughout Japanese history well into the twentieth century.

The new leadership from the Satsuma and Choshu clans was determined to bring Japan into the modern world as rapidly as possible.

They had used modern rifle companies to defeat the Shogun's troops and clearly understood that if Japan were to compete with European powers, it would have to remake its entire society.

The samurai class was abolished as warriors, and a new conscript army was created to defend the nation. A modern army and navy were created, trained and equipped with modern weapons. All the trappings of the old shogunate system were eliminated, and scores of young men were sent abroad to discover how other nations operated and to bring new ideas back home to be implemented. They adopted countless ideas and methods from the Western world in order to gain sufficient strength to resist the ever growing military strength of the industrial powers in the West, beating them at their own game.

Former daimyos were offered positions in the government and gained a steady income in lieu of their previous uncertain income based on the production of rice. Since there was a great need for new industries in manufacturing, trade, finance and supplying raw materials, the government created a highly centralized society which offered many opportunities for individuals to build fortunes. These opportunities were enhanced by a government policy of granting exclusive contracts for new industries along with financial assistance, cheap loans and protection from domestic competition. Such policies served as great enticements for former daimyos, who became quite successful businessmen.

Since they saw they had fallen so far behind the West, the leaders were convinced that if they were to survive in the modern world, they would have to adopt new techniques of production and practices of governing. They copied infrastructure as varied as the Philadelphia sewage system and the U.S. National Banking System. The latter, however, did not prove to be successful and was soon dropped for another system. The Bank of Japan controlled not only the national currency but served to fund much of the industrial expansion. It is worthy of note that other than two small loans from Great Britain in the first decade of the Meiji period, the Japanese did not have to borrow from foreign sources as they expanded their economy.

They did borrow their political system, finding a philosophy in the new constitution of the recently unified German state was to their liking. The final result was the Meiji Constitution, which was granted to the people on February 11, 1889, as a way of commemorating the founding of Japan by the Sun Goddess in 660 B.C.

The committee drafting the constitution was chaired by Ito Hirobumi, who had been one of the young men sent abroad almost immediately after the restoration. He went to Western Europe, and after several months he decided that the recently created Prussian-style document adopted by the newly unified German nation was best suited for Japan. At Ito's request, the government asked that a German scholar, H. K. Roessler, be invited to assist in the drafting of the new political document. After more than two year's effort, the document was completed. When asked about his work on the document, Roessler replied that he was sure there were words in the constitution that were not his, but he was not sure he could find any.

The Meiji Constitution

The Emperor was supreme and considered a divinity who had "granted" this gift to the nation. While the constitution stated that all power rested in the hands of the emperor, in reality he was a figurehead whose name was used by the political leadership. The structure of the new government offered a façade of representative democracy, but it provided that the national government cabinet be required to have ministers of the army and navy appointed by those services and that no government could exist without these two positions filled. This meant that if the military leadership did not like the budget allocations for that year, it could order the two ministers to resign, which automatically collapsed the existing cabinet.

This document had limited suffrage in that only males paying a certain tax would be eligible to vote. It created a bicameral legislative system with a House of Lords and a lower House of Representatives. The leaders from Choshu and Satsuma clans, along with others, appointed themselves as titled nobility to populate the House of Lords.

The former council of elders concept from the days of the shogunate was continued. It was called the Genro, and it was also dominated by the leaders from Choshu and Satsuma, and the saying soon began to be heard that the Emperor should not do anything without first asking the Genro.

Much is made of the Meiji Constitution, but very little attention was paid to the Imperial Rescript to soldiers and sailors. The Imperial Rescript, written by General Yamagata, created a special relationship between Japanese military forces and the Emperor and was formally presented on January 4, 1882. This signified that the armed forces were personally responsible to the Emperor. When this was presented to the Japanese armed forces personally by Emperor Meiji in 1882, it signified that all military forces report directly to the Imperial Court and not the Japanese Diet. This rescript was read aloud to all military forces no fewer than three times per week and included over 2700 characters or words, which had to be memorized by all. From what I was told by Japanese officers and noncoms , it was very effective in urging the troops to fight to the last and that to die for the Emperor was the most honorable way to die.

The military was told also in the document that they should ignore public opinions and avoid being involved in any political activity. Yamagata's influence permeates the content of this document. His conviction that the military path was the only path which could help his nation achieve its goals of being a world power representing the Far East.

A small number of samurai who wanted to remain the supreme class kept on for several years, until the new conscript army with modern weapons wiped out most of the remaining members. The rest were paid a very small stipend to totally disband. Traditions about the old samurai families and their swords persist even into this century. A 1980 survey of industrial, banking, trading and political leadership showed that nearly 30% still claimed descent from samurai families.

Economic growth

During the first two decades of the new regime, growth in agriculture and commerce overshadowed industrial growth. By 1880, agricultural acreage increased by 7% and the average yield per acre by 21%. Total farm output doubled in 25 years, a remarkable achievement. In the industrial areas, the government took the lead in building shipyards at Yokuksuka, Nagasaki and Kobe. Government-owned factories in Tokyo and Osaka borrowed technology from abroad to smelt iron and cast cannon. Factories manufacturing rifles, ammunition and gun powder were up and running full blast by 1880.

Quite fortunately for the incoming government, there was a great silk blight in Europe in 1869, leading to a great demand for Japanese silk. This very quickly became Japan's major export by 1880, when exports of silk made up 43% of outgoing Japanese products. Consequently, by 1885 Japan had achieved a favorable balance of trade for its national economy.

During the 1870s, inflation was rampant, and paper currency was worth about half of its face value. A former samurai, Baron Matsukata, became minister of finance. To solve the problem, the government sold off its industrial ventures at discounts from 11% to 90% of their true value. There were no bids in the trade, and everything went to insiders. Within a few years, there were giant corporations known as the zaibatsu, or financial cliques.

The Bank of Japan was in full operation by 1882 and within four years the international financial system was operating in the black insofar as government activities were concerned.

Another major area of concern for the leadership was to meet the requirements of having a conscript army. It needed to have recruits that were literate and had at least a minimum level of education. The leadership determined that it would use the French model in establishing a nationwide system. It made the first 16 months of school compulsory in 1880, and this was shortly extended to three years. By 1907, six years were required, and it was estimated at that time that 95% of all children in the nation were attending school. Schools were coeducational through the first six years, the academic middle school for boys had a five-year curriculum and there were some secondary schools for girls from richer families. The highest school for boys was three years in attendance, and a medical degree required four years to gain a license.

The philosophy underlying the great efforts put forth to create a modern nation was based on the almost universal agreement that the problems facing Japan domestically required an aggressive foreign policy. Its total lack of mineral resources, oil, and limited agricultural lands made it obvious to many Japanese that the economy could never grow without being able to obtain the raw materials necessary for manufacturing at home. It was equally necessary that the nation had to export finished products far beyond anything it they had done before to maintain a balanced economy.

The military

In 1900, Japan furnished the largest military contingent for the relief of foreign diplomats in China to put down the Boxer Rebellion. The inordinately large Japanese contingent of 72,000 troops sent was meant to impress the other nations of Japanese power.

The national leadership was firmly convinced Japan was the Asiatic country that had developed sufficiently to be able to have a joint treaty with the greatest naval power in the world, Great Britain. The Anglo-Japanese Treaty of 1901 not only recognized Japan's modernization drives in the last third of the previous century, it also relieved some naval defense concerns of Great Britain.

The military strength of the nation increased rapidly as the early emphasis put upon creating manufacturing modern equipment and materials and conscription created a rapidly expanding army and navy. The outstanding leader of the Japanese military system was Yamagata Aritomo, who had been born in the Choshu domain in 1838. He came from a lower-ranking samurai family. During his early days in school, he devoted his energies to an underground movement to overthrow the shogunate.

He and Tsugumichi Saigo were selected to research European military systems. He was very impressed with the striking success of the Prussian army and with the development under way to transform the new Germany from an agricultural economy into one that was an industrial and military power.

He was totally dedicated to making Japan a major military power. He organized a national army for Japan upon his return, controlled the legislation leading to conscription and personally led the first troops, numbering 10,000. He used these troops to put down the last samurai uprising in Kyushu in 1876. One of the leaders of the samurai in this uprising was his friend Saigo, who was killed in the battle. Yamagata requested that Saigo's severed head be brought to him. He then proceeded to meditate with his friend's head in his hands.

He became a member of the Genro for over 30 years, and held several very important government posts, serving as prime minister on two separate occasions, and one for the four years just prior to the proclamation of the Meiji Constitution.

In 1883 he was appointed Lord Chancellor, the highest bureaucratic position in the nation. He was president of the Privy Council from 1893-94 and from 1905 until his death in 1922. As Minister of War, he pushed through legislation which created the Imperial Japanese Army General Staff, which became the basis for his great political power. He was the commanding general in the Sino-Japanese War in 1894-1895, which resulted in China giving away all rights in Korea. Over the next few years, the Japanese military expanded its control over the Korean peninsula, and in 1910 Japan formally annexed Korea, with very little attention paid to the action by the world diplomatic community.

His greatest political enemy was Ito Hirobumi, who had shared with him a place on the constitutional committee. Ito fully understood the significance of adopting a Prussian-style constitution that provided for a modern Japan dominated by the military and industrial leaders. At the same time, he was convinced that the political leadership of the country should be carried out by elected officials. He formed a political party called the Seiyukai in the 1890s whose goal was to establish a precedent by giving the civilian parties actual control of the nation. Ito and Yamagata fought each other politically until Ito's death in 1909, when Yamagata became the most important and powerful political figure in the nation.

Over the next 12 or 13 years, Yamagata consolidated his political power. He had outlasted Ito and consequently firmly placed Japan in the control of the military and political forces of the nation. This influence was manifested during the 1930s in Japan's pre-war and wartime leadership. Yamagata is considered the father of the Japanese armed forces. There is no question as to the extent of his influence. He was full of plans for expanding the Japanese Empire, using the armed forces of his nation to obtain sources of raw material, fuel and markets for Japanese finished products throughout the Eastern Hemisphere. The tragedy for Japan and the world, particularly East Asian Nations and Indonesia, was that peaceful diplomacy and mutual trade benefits were ignored in favor of brute force.

Emperor Meiji died in 1911, the year the Anglo-Japanese Treaty was extended. The leaders of the Meiji era could look back and celebrate their outstanding achievements. They had remade the entire structure of Japan from that of a highly centralized feudal state into a modern nation in only 40 years. They had established a new political system with the trappings of a modern state and almost totally created a modern industrialized base to gain respect throughout the world. The alliance with Great Britain, extended in 1911, was recognition of equality with at the time the most powerful naval power on the planet. They also succeeded in removing the extraterritorial clauses from all treaties with the Western Powers through reforming their judicial processes.

4

THE CULTURE OF JAPAN

Japan's geography and early development played a key role in determining the character and culture of its people. Overall, there is a great cultural homogeneity and only in the small population in the northern island of Hokkaido are there citizens who are distinctly unique in their physical appearance. The 20,000 Ainu are quite different and are the major population from which sumo wrestlers are drawn. Since the geographic environment is relatively small and generally uniform, in the population centers there is little difference in the speech patterns. There are some who will say that the natives of Kyushu, the southernmost of the main four islands, have a more distinct accent.

Perhaps one of the most evident aspects of Japanese culture is the role of hierarchy. Almost from the beginning of Japanese society, there was a belief that differences in rank and status have always been and always will be. As far back as the Wei Chronicles, Chinese scholars emphasized the great respect the Japanese had for gradations of rank as they described relations between the superior and inferior individuals in Japanese culture. And even several centuries later, Will Adams commented on Japan's rigid social order and the firm government control.

The political arrangement in Japanese society has been based on the idea for many centuries that power is hereditary and aristocratic rule is the standard practice. The Japanese are constantly seeking to live according to their status. They tend to act according to their age and position in society at all times, and as these factors change, it affects their self identification. They frequently use titles in addressing others which differ as positions or age change. On occasion, people hire kuromaku, "political wire pullers," to influence political decisions through direct or indirect connections related to wealth, to position and, at one time, to ties to violence. The third factor had almost completely disappeared in the latter part of the last century.

Despite the strong and continuing pressure for citizens to conform to their status in life, the Japanese still retained a degree of individualism that should not be overlooked. The great majority of Japanese individuals go through a childhood where they are quite spoiled by their parents through a rebellious youth to become absolutely conformist adults.

Despite the pressure, there are still many areas where Japanese are able to emphasize their own unique capabilities and interests. There are a variety of ways in which the Japanese counteract the great pressure to conform, whether it is in politics or business or the workplace.

The economic spread between the rich and poor was wide in the latter part of the Meiji era and prior to World War I and World War II. But the devastation of World War II went a long way to wipe out much of the accumulated wealth in Japan. There continues to be a high inheritance tax which also tends to discourage the accumulation of great wealth. Most Japanese in our current economy will respond to any question concerning their economic class by saying they belong to the middle class nine times out of 10.

There are now fewer class divisions, and over the centuries the rigidity of social arrangements has relaxed following the start of the modern Meiji period. The distinction between a samurai family and commoners is less meaningful with each generation. There is still, however, a distinction maintained between nobility and commoners. The last analysis of this division was in the last decade in which a study demonstrated that nearly 40% of business executives identified themselves as being of samurai descent.

The group mentality

Another outstanding feature of the Japanese culture is its formation around group preferences and ideals. Many writers have stated that Japanese society is basically a group society, and with that I have no argument. The highly crowded living conditions in most Japanese cities contribute to the development of groupism as a way of life. The linchpin to a successful happy life is to be in harmony with those around you.

Usually, Japanese groups are combinations of equals in a hierarchical arrangement; businessmen of the same age would constitute a group. Almost all groups are divided into leaders and followers. This simply reflects the practice in Japanese families.

Others note that Japanese use their family first and then the individual name. It is more important for the Japanese to know the family from which a person comes than to know who an individual is, as is common in our society. Respect for the elderly and family names are therefore eternal elements in Japanese society.

The ideal is for individuals to act their age, so their behaviors change with their number of years.

From a very early age, Japanese children are given almost total freedom to move about in any location and do whatever strikes them as being interesting. I remember one occasion when a Japanese family was visiting my home in the United States, and we went to a moderately priced restaurant for dinner. They had a young boy who was two years old at the time. During the course of the meal, which I'm sure he did not find very interesting, he proceeded to climb over the booth and crawl on top of it about every five or 10 minutes. In each and every instance his parents simply ignored the child's behavior or patted him on the back and told him what a good boy he was. This behavior was rather surprising, since the Japanese are usually very careful about how they behave in public. I surmise from what I have observed that Japanese children are in a sense spoiled by their mothers and permitted to do almost anything. This may explain some of the behavior as children start school at an early age.

When they are in the early elementary grades there are certain routine steps that are taken which really introduce the student to the idea of working as a team or a group. The chairs are set in rows in the elementary classroom, and the teacher will designate one row with a responsibility for that week. They usually eat their school-prepared lunch in their classrooms, and at the appointed time the various teams of students perform certain functions in the lunch hour. One team will rearrange the chairs and desks in the room for eating, another will see that the food is distributed, a third group might well provide the drinks brought to the desk of each student. The fourth and fifth groups see to it that the leftover food and materials are put back on the cart and rearrange the chairs after making sure that everything has been cleaned up.

At the end of the week, the teacher spends a few minutes reviewing the activities of the current week and asks the students which team did the most outstanding job. That team will receive recognition from the teacher and perhaps some small reward. On some occasions, the teacher engages the students in discussing what is considered to be efficient in working as a group effort or whether certain behavior diminishes the efficiency and smoothness of how the team operates.

Even in the current century modern styles of dress and behavior among the upcoming generation sustain the practice of doing things in groups. I noted youthful protesters wore similar clothing, sometimes outrageous, and congregated together while trying to show their contempt for some of the practices from earlier times. Some of these ideas may have been introduced during the Occupation after World War II, but many resulted from the worldwide media exposure of the latest fads in modern attire and music.

Another demonstration of the emphasis placed on group behavior or group team action occurs when one group enters into an athletic competition and does particularly well. One teacher explained to me that her fifth-grade class had been entered into a swimming competition with other fifth-grade classes in the elementary schools of the city where she was teaching. One of the young boys was an extraordinary swimmer, and out of the eight different competitions he placed first in five of them. It was obvious that this class was going to be awarded the swimming championship banner for that particular year.

When the principal of the school made the announcement and awarded the banner to this particular fifth-grade class, he did not mention the young boy who had won the five medals but congratulated the entire class on their outstanding performance in the swimming competition. What was even more significant was that the young man who had won all of the medals considered this to be very proper and did not feel in any way that he had been slighted despite his great achievements. The fact that it was his team or class that received the award was merit enough for all. The constant attention to group activities continues throughout the entire educational system.

At the collegiate level, Japanese educational structures are different than those in the United States. The American structural units are geared to separate academic disciplines, such as the Department of English or Physics or any discipline. The faculty in each department functions in such a way through assignments and teaching specific skills to students.

In the Japanese system, particularly at the graduate level, a departmental structure does not exist. Japanese structure revolves around given individuals who have the rank of full professor. This individual is in charge of a particular academic specialty within a broad discipline and has assistant professors and graduate students to assist in performing his duties. The senior professor selects his assistant staff and graduate students, assigns them the necessary responsibilities and directs their research efforts and teaching tasks. He is responsible for evaluating the performance of his students and staff and in many ways operates almost as an individual enterprise.

This contrasts markedly with the colleges in the United States where academic departments determine the content and progress of faculty and students through departmental meetings made up of committees which handle evaluations, promotions, curricular innovations, and the physical and research needs of the faculty in that department.

The consequence of the Japanese system is that it continues the reliance of the individual going through an educational process from elementary school to universities of people upon an authority figure. In elementary schools, the children line up in a formation on the school grounds every morning and are greeted by a principal or supervisor of the institution. This represents the first step in training students to respect an authority figure. Along the way, processes contribute to the Japanese respect for those who are in a higher status or to whom they are responsible for their jobs or positions regardless of whether it is in civilian life or the military. There have been some modifications of the system in the last decade. During the twentieth century, there was a gradual shift from hereditary hierarchy as a source of power to an educational system which increased steadily the status of individuals. This in turn provided greater mobility in social circles, business and probably in government officialdom.

The Japanese have individual rights according to the 1947 Occupation-led revision of their constitution, and these rights are enforceable through the Supreme Court of the land. The Japanese may appreciate these rights, but they are by no means rugged individualists in a general sense. Each Japanese may have a particular hobby, unique skill or artistic flair through which they express their individuality, but they are basically individuals who identify with groups. If a Japanese citizen has a job or position, he or she will identify with the company and demonstrate strong loyalty and pride and security in the company group. Even large businesses tend to get into groups along with similar organizations such as the Keidanren.

Probably the largest organization in the nation is the Soka Gakkai. With over 10 to 12 million members, it was formed on a national basis just to provide groups for people who do not belong to groups.

This is probably a result of having three or more generations of a family living together so that to sustain harmony it is important to recognize the desires of others. In many ways this is simply a continuation of the early agricultural villages which functioned as a unified whole in order to produce a satisfactory and sufficient rice crop every year. The Japanese continue to sustain their national culture and historical customs into the twenty-first century.

A travel group, for example, might end up planning a trip to an area in South America with several members of the group not wanting to go there at all. But for the sake of harmony, they say nothing and go along with the majority voice in their group. This is considered to be highly commendable in Japanese society and is a demonstration of great inner strength.

If you notice in large American airports or around the world, the Japanese usually travel in groups and stay clustered together until their leader has decided which direction they should go and what they should do. I have found in my travels that there are very few Japanese families that travel by themselves. This may be due to language difficulties or to simply their past practices of traveling in groups. In the past few years I have noticed more smaller groups traveling abroad.

Outliers

There are some elements of the population who for one reason or another do not fit into the overwhelming majority of the population. They tend to aggregate in the slum areas of the major cities. While there are still yakuza, or organized gangs, in the major Japanese cities, they do not behave as criminal gangs would in our society. The local police have substations scattered in many areas of the large cities and are in close contact with individuals in some of these yakuza. It is interesting to note that the local police forces are ultimately under the control of the Ministry of Home Affairs, which allows the central government to have direct management of local law enforcement agencies in times of crisis.

For others, the entertainment world known as the mizu-shobai still functions in large urban centers. Bargirls still perform various forms of prostitution despite the fact that this has been outlawed since the end of World War II. There are bars, discos, floor shows and sing-along places, karaoke, which serve as safety valves for the distraught individual who is fed up with a particular situation either at work or in one of their numerous societies. In many bars located around the business areas, there would be a "mama-san" who ran the establishment and became a confidante of many a frustrated Japanese businessman who had become exasperated with some situation, either at work or at home. Mama-sans would lend a willing ear to the outpouring of the individual, who would be also having a few drinks.

I remember an event which reflects the struggle between the desires of the individual and the social requirements of his position. I was in a high location one afternoon just sitting and enjoying scenery when I heard the loud roar of a motorcycle coming up the small road. The occupant stopped on a small mesa and began pacing back and forth, obviously very upset and quite angry. He alternated for probably 15 or 20 minutes between pacing and sitting down almost with his head between his knees. Finally he stood up, threw his arms up in the air and shouted "baka" and then got back on his bike and rode quietly back down the hill.

Japanese society is very tolerant of drunkenness and is quite generous in overlooking the behavior of individuals under the influence. I witnessed on one occasion a quite tipsy individual wearing a business suit coming out of a bar. He attempted to cross the street even though traffic was quite heavy. He moved around a few cars, and a policeman who was standing by simply blew his whistle and stopped traffic while the inebriated person managed to get to the other side of the street. The policeman actually helped him over the curb without saying a word and let the man continue on his way.

One effect of the island nation's condensed amount of land is seen in its approach to art. In addition to the basic needs of the nation to extract as much food from the small arable areas in the valleys and from the sea around the island nation, the society concentrated its artistic development on small areas of land for use as garden plots, and the decoration of collateral areas to express their artistic sensitivity in beautiful landscape designs. Even today, garden areas in parks and public areas are carefully sculpted to produce attractive areas. Temple grounds also homes for various kinds of design, and many use sand formations as the material. The attention to detail in every artistic undertaking has become a trademark of Japanese culture recognized around the world. This artistic cultural development extended to include clothing, costuming, and even stage productions. Thus, there are intriguing national dramas which reflect the deepest feelings of its people. *The Tales of the 47 Ronin* stands out as the quintessential production of Japanese culture, but several centuries before that, there were similar tales that reflect ideals of their society.

The development of the Noh dramatic style is uniquely Japanese and reflects the remarkable skills of artistic designers in theatrical productions. These techniques and attention to the details and historic backgrounds gradually became more or less concentrated in several special families who passed their knowledge only to members of their families. The result is a near monopoly status of these art forms and acting techniques.

5

❧

JAPAN IN THE TWENTIETH CENTURY

The rapid transformation of Japan from a highly centralized feudal state, at least theoretically, and its appearance in the Far East as a significant player in diplomacy coincided with the advent of the twentieth century.

The United States had become a Pacific power with the acquisitions of the Philippines and Guam as part of the Treaty of Paris ending the Spanish-American War in 1898. The rise of American influence in the area was exercised almost immediately. . The Japanese had kept China from having claims on the Korean Peninsula in the Treaty of Shimonoseki in 1895, and it was continuing its drive to build a strong army and navy. The U.S. Secretary of State, John Hay, had decided that the stability of the East Asian area would be gravely disturbed if the continuing dismantling of China were to continue.

Hay had become aware of the rise of Chinese nationalist movements, thanks to the British ambassador to China, Lord Beresford, who had been a friend of Hay for some years. The British Foreign Office had ordered Lord Beresford to return to London by using an indirect route, crossing the Pacific and taking a train across the United States, to inform Hay personally of British concerns about China. Great Britain had been increasingly aware of German naval rearmament programs and felt it necessary to bring the major part of the British Far Eastern fleet back to its home waters. The introduction of the dreadnaught style battleships by Germany placed a severe strain on the British budget, since the British had decided to match the German production.

Consequently, Lord Beresford's visit was more than a personal one; it was an attempt on the part of the British government to sustain its possessions in the Far East by obtaining American willingness to maintain the status quo. Following these talks, Hay adopted the idea of having all the major nations with interests in the Far East agree to maintain the territorial integrity of China.

By this time, several European nations had secured special rights in Chinese ports, where they were developing their own special spheres of influence. This meant that the European powers would take control an area surrounding a Chinese port, over which they acquired special police powers, collection of duties and tariffs, and control of the budgets of their sphere. The Chinese government was so disorganized that local warlords ignored the central government and negotiated with these other nations, and the situation grew steadily worse. Hay sent a formal statement to the nations involved in the Far East and asked if they would have any objections to agreeing that all nations would maintain and preserve Chinese territorial integrity.

Since no nation wanted to appear as an aggressor before world opinion, no one raised any objections. On September 1, 1899, Hay issued the first of the Open Door Notes, stating that all the nations had agreed to this policy. Shortly thereafter, he discovered a loophole whereby a local Chinese governor could act as a front for the controlling foreign power. Therefore, on July 4, 1900, he issued a second note declaring that all nations had agreed to also sustain Chinese administrative integrity. These two notes became the basis of American foreign policy until the attack on Pearl Harbor.

Fundamentally, the Open Door Policy tried to place a brake on the numerous efforts of the modern nations to gain special advantages in China and East Asia. The sequence of developments in a takeover of these still underdeveloped countries usually involved starting with discovery of an area for trade, then establishing ever increasing controls, and finally annexing the area as a colony. These imperialist steps were apparently justified in the eyes of the western political leaders, who moved rapidly from opening trade relations with an area to the establishment of a sphere of influence. At this stage, the foreign power would have exclusive trading rights and as well as economic and political control. Most of the colonial powers were well advanced in this process when Hay's Open Door Policy was introduced. Even the U.S. had had a special interest in Fukien Province a year later and paid only lip service to the Open Door.

Despite the issuance of the Open Door notes, the British, still seeking assurances that their interests would be protected in the event of war in Europe, entered into a secret agreement with Japan the next year which basically stated that Japan and Great Britain would come to each other's assistance in the event of any attack. This Anglo-Japanese Pact was to run for 10 years, at which time it was renewed for another 10 years.

Like the Monroe Doctrine of the early nineteenth century, the Open Door Policy became a justification for the U.S. to be dealing with a wide range of issues which arose in the succeeding years. Each was insofar as possible used to further American interests under the guise of a noble gesture to protect underdeveloped areas in both the Western and Eastern hemispheres from what we deemed to be foreign intervention. Each of the two Open Door Notes was eventually seen to be almost an international law. While not realizing it at the time, the United States would become the enforcer of these documents covering both the Western Hemisphere and the Far East.

After the turn of the twentieth century, numerous issues arose between Japan and the United States. One was the inflow of immigrants from Japan in the first decade, causing increasing unrest in the western states, who complained about the impact these foreigners were having on their culture. Stories were repeated about the unhealthiness of having older Japanese male students enrolling in American public schools to learn English. They were deemed to be a bad influence on the children in our elementary schools. This was especially decried in San Francisco, but an investigation later revealed that in the entire San Francisco public school system there were only two Japanese who were 18 or 19 enrolled in the elementary grades.

Public outcries against continued immigration were raised. Elihu Root, the U.S. Secretary of State, and the Japanese negotiator, Takahira Kogoro, worked out an agreement released in 1908 that was admittedly a face-saving device for Japan. In effect, the United States and Japan agreed that the latter government would take steps to stop immigration to the American mainland. The United States agreed that no language would be used to disparage members of the yellow race and that the San Francisco school board would make adjustments to insure that immigrant students could attend its schools.

Political unrest in Tsarist Russia in the early years of the twentieth century afforded Japan another opportunity to expand its influence on the mainland of Asia. The unannounced attack on the Russian fleet in Port Arthur on the tip of the Liaotung peninsula set off the Russo-Japanese war of 1904-1905. The war ended with the Treaty of Portsmouth, mediated by U.S. President Theodore Roosevelt. The British refusal to permit the Russian Baltic Fleet to use the Suez Canal during the war led to a great naval victory for Japan over an exhausted Russian fleet in the Tsushima Straits west of the Japanese mainland. The terms of the treaty provided that Russia would give up all claims to the Korean Peninsula.

But Count Witte, the Russian representative, refused to pay any indemnity. When the news of the treaty provisions was published in Japan, there were widespread demonstrations over the failure to obtain any reparations from Russia. The Japanese effort in the conduct of the war had been enormous, and the expectation was that the costly drain on its financial reserves would be replenished by these reparations. Neither side in the conflict was satisfied with the results, which boded ill for future relationships between the two nations. The mediation of the Russo-Japanese War in 1905 became an irritant to some Japanese, since the lack of any financial indemnity from Russia was partially laid at the feet of Theodore Roosevelt's intervention.

Serious challenges

While these irritants did not involve any military action on the part of the United States, a far more serious challenge arose during World War I. The outbreak of the war in late July, 1914, presented another opportunity for Japan to further its influence in the Far East and the Pacific Ocean area. In line with the terms of the Anglo-Japanese Pact, the Japanese army seized the Shantung peninsula, which had been under German control. The small German garrison did not put up any opposition as the Japanese army took control. This was immediately followed by Japanese naval forces seizing all German island colonies in the Pacific Ocean area, both north and south of the equator. I remember talking in German with a native chief, called Ellissan, in the Kwajalein Islands, since he spoke no English or Japanese. The justification for these seizures was that Japan had carried out its obligations under the agreement with Great Britain.

The great struggle in Europe also afforded Japan an opportunity for expansion into China. In 1915, Japan presented the Chinese government with a list of 21 demands, divided into five distinct groups. The Japanese insisted on the confidential nature of these negotiations, by which Japan was to take over police powers, finances, taxing authority, foreign policy and control of import and export trade. For all intents and purposes, if the Chinese government had accepted these demands, China would have become a colony of Japan.

The Chinese were warned that these matters were to be kept totally confidential. A young Chinese diplomat, however, reported the existence of the demands to the United States and pleaded for assistance in this matter. The first inquiries made to Japan by the United States were rejected out of hand. They denied the existence of any requests but finally stated there had been some correspondence between the two nations attempting to resolve some issues.

The Japanese pressure on the Chinese government to yield to the 21 Demands while keeping their negotiations secret was a clear indication that Japan understood the implications of the Open Door Policy and sought to use the abnormal realities of the world at war The Japanese were also keenly aware that the rise of Chinese nationalism in the first two decades of the twentieth century created an urgency for Japan to take action.

The U.S. State Department was informed by the Chinese ambassador, Wellington Koo, that the 21 demands had been placed in five classifications and requested American support. At first the Japanese insisted that there were only four major categories. They apparently knew nothing of the fifth section which would have given Japan nearly total control of the Chinese mainland.

After 16 months of negotiations, the Lansing-Ishii Letters of Agreement were signed as simply an understanding between the two nations. This four-paragraph statement constituted further ambiguous language which permitted each nation to claim that it had achieved its objectives. Our Secretary of State, Robert Lansing, waved the document in the air when reporting to the U.S. Senate and cited the first part which declared that both parties reaffirmed their support of the Open Door. Lansing claimed that this was a diplomatic victory for the United States. His counterpart, Viscount Ishii, informed his countrymen that it was a diplomatic victory for Japan, since the third paragraph stated that the United States understood that the territorial propinquity of Japan to China might require Japan to take this into consideration when dealing with China. To the Japanese, this represented a far deeper meaning. They interpreted this to mean that the United States would not go to war for the benefit of the Chinese. It simply placed another log on the incendiary relationship between the two nations.

Bluntly analyzed, neither of the parties to this agreement wanted to fight over the status of China. The diplomatic doubletalk in the agreement provided a face-saving device for both Japan and the U.S. The Great War in Europe was deemed to be of far greater importance. Very real tensions had existed between Japan and the United States, and the peaceful resolution of the matter was hailed by both sides as a great victory. Viscount Ishii was treated to a great celebration in Honolulu on his trip back to Japan for his participation in the negotiations.

World War I

Both China and Japan entered World War I on the side of the Allies. The Japanese used the opportunity to gain control of German islands in the Pacific and the Chinese paid for some limited ambulance services in France as a token of its support.

The harsh reality of World War I is hard to overstate. The concert of Europe was wracked from stem to stern in almost every aspect of human existence. Trench warfare was marked on many occasions by hand-to-hand combat and exposure to extremes of temperature. The death toll of the combatants in that generation eliminated so many men of military age that the political, social and economic consequences bordered on disaster. The French expression that its national assembly was in reality a Horizon Blue chamber referred to the ages of the representatives who continued in office because there were insufficient numbers of younger people to take their place. The appointment of Raymond Poincare as premier in 1926 at age 66 simply underscored the situation in which the French people found themselves.

The number of casualties suffered in the European struggles was greater than anyone had ever imagined was possible. Entire portions of some areas, where the fighting had been prolonged and severe, were no longer suitable for habitation. Some villages were entirely destroyed, and the leftover ammunition, shells, and land mines made even agricultural efforts very dangerous. Shopping centers in many European cities offered specialized shoes that were made for victims crippled by the war. There was special seating on public transportation for veterans. The continuous appearance of wounded vets trying to get around had a depressing effect on the general public mood and atmosphere in many countries.

The great struggle in the Verdun, made famous by General Phillipe Petain's pronouncement, "They shall not pass," resulted in nearly 1,500,000 deaths of German and French soldiers. A pallor hung low over the area for years, and the physical damage resulting from the struggle was in some instances never improved or removed.

Added to the terrible loss of life in ground warfare was the dawn of a new era of weaponry which promised to be even more efficient in killing enemy troops. The advent of poison gas used on a wide scale was another deadly innovation of World War I. The introduction of submarines proved to be quite effective in sinking enemy ships transporting military goods from one continent to another. The old professional armies of the previous century gave way to widespread drafting of ordinary citizens to be quickly trained and thrown into battle. These and many other innovations were very costly in terms of human life and contributed to the difficulty encountered at the Versailles Conference ending World War I, which labored to produce a peace treaty that determined who would control nearly 80 to 90% of the earth's surface. New countries were formed, names of others were changed, and a mandate system was created to deal with problematic areas which did not have existing governments. Both Japan and China sought assurances that their interests would be protected.

As part of this process of handling German colonial areas, agreement was reached between Japan and Great Britain that provided that all former German islands south of the equator were given to the British and all north of that line assigned to Japan as mandated areas. The mandate system required that the controlling nation attend to the well being of the native inhabitants and establish a local government to provide for future independence. Regular inspections by League of Nation officials were to oversee the actions of Japan and Great Britain in the former German colonies. It must be noted that the Japanese were able to avoid any inspection of their islands through one delaying tactic or another. Some of these islands were indeed fortified by Japan, a fact which the U.S. verified the hard way in the Pacific Theater.

Attempts at peace

Out of the destruction of World War I, there were numerous suggestions about how to prevent such an awful struggle from ever occurring again. The most common recommendation was for the nations of the world to adopt a disarmament plan. Although the United States Senate refused to ratify the disarmament treaty, there was strong support for various disarmament proposals.

President Wilson's strong desire to establish a League of Nations to keep the peace met with opposition in our Senate. His position was weakened at Versailles when he voted against a Japanese-originated resolution eliminating all discrimination against members of the yellow race. President Wilson obviously was thinking if he had voted for the resolution it would cost him support from western senators who would vote against the creation of the League of Nations.

This became another log on the fires of Japanese public opinion against the United States and was frequently cited by Japanese war hawks in the 1930s. President Woodrow Wilson predicted while in Colorado shortly before his stroke that if the nations of the world did not use the League of Nations, we would have another world war in 20 years.

His conviction that this would happen may have grown out of the myriad problems facing the delegates who were trying to restore order in 1919. As Wilson crawled over the huge map of Europe, drawing lines based on the ideas of self-determination and defensible frontiers as a guarantee of a peaceful post-war, little attention was paid to the far Pacific nations and colonies. The failure of the Senate to ratify the treaty has been blamed for the chaos which followed in the next two decades. In retrospect, the aspirations of people all over the globe had been stirred by the depth and scope of the death toll and suffering in World War I which led to actions and reactions throughout the world.

The mandate system of the League was a noble gesture at best. Within 15 years Great Britain and France had given up on their responsibilities in the Middle East and simply abandoned them in spite of the need for supervision in many areas. The disastrous effects of World War I led to extremist ideologies springing up in Europe, the Middle East and the Far East. The legacy of the first world war included the rise of communism in Russia and fascism in Europe and South American countries.

The Washington Conference on Disarmament in 1921-1922 produced three major agreements known as the Four-, Five-, and Nine-Power Pacts. U.S. Secretary of State Charles Evans Hughes had opened the sessions with a stunning and comprehensive review as to the status of naval armaments both afloat and under construction throughout the world. He urged the delegates to formally agree to reduce their arms, his assumption being that wars had been caused by nations building up huge forces at great cost and was prone to take military action to resolve problems rather than utilize diplomatic channels. The reduction of arms was carried out with moderate success almost without thinking about the location of naval bases in strategic parts of the world. The U.S., Great Britain and Japan apportioned their naval power in a proportion of 5:5:3 though later this was changed to a ratio of 10:10:7, improving Japan's status.

The Japanese drive to acquire more resources on the Asian mainland led to the Mukden incident in 1931. Under the terms of the Treaty of Portsmouth between Russia and Japan, the Japanese became the dominant force in southern Manchuria. The rise of the Kuomintang movement under General Chiang Kai Shek, stressing Chinese nationalism, was considered a threat to Japan's aims of exploiting the mineral resources of Manchuria. Japanese diplomats started exerting pressure on General Hsuch-Hang; they found him to be a strong supporter of the Chinese nationalist movement and refused to consider Japanese demands.

In September of 1931, a bomb exploded on the railway near

Mukden, and despite any evidence as to its source, it served as an excuse for the Japanese army to occupy the southern part of Manchuria. China appealed to the League of Nations, and the General Assembly authorized an investigative commission headed by Lord Lytton of Great Britain to act as the chair.

The commission worked for nearly a year to ascertain the facts of the incident. Despite objections by the Japanese cabinet and assurances given to the League of Nations that it would withdraw its troops, the Japanese army overran all of Manchuria, set up a puppet government and renamed the new state of Manchukuo in the early months of 1932.

The Lytton Commission finished its work and reported to the League General Assembly in December, 1932. Its report charged Japan as being responsible for the incident. The report cited Japan as the aggressor and should withdraw its troops and pay an indemnity to China.

The General Assembly considered the report for 30 days and voted unanimously to accept the report and called on Japan to make amends. Six weeks later in March, 1933, the Japanese ambassador to the League of Nations complained that his nation had fully cooperated with the Lytton Commission but totally disagreed with its finding, walked out of the session and the League of Nations. Thus, Japan was the first nation to leave the League of Nations.

Henry Stimson, the U.S. Secretary of State, issued a policy statement following the departure of Japan from the League which became known as the Stimson Doctrine. It stated that "the United States would not accept the seizure of territory through the use of force." He further added this country would retain freedom of action concerning such developments. In effect, Stimson was loading a pistol pointed at Japan which we could use whenever we wished.

6

THE BEGINNINGS OF WAR

While the Tokyo government made no public statement concerning Stimson's policy, the Japanese press contained strong criticism of the posture of the United States. The major thrust of these articles compared the fully developed status of the United States with that of Japan, pointing out that their nation was still developing its industries. It was unfair of the Americans to condemn the Japanese for striving to enhance their economic growth so that they could enjoy many commodities like the United States.

The British and French governments simply walked away from their mandate responsibilities in the Near East, and the Japanese proceeded to secretly arm many of the former German islands in the Pacific north of the equator for which they had mandate responsibilities under the League of Nations. When the Japanese left the League in March, 1933, not too much attention was paid. Only later, when the rest of the Axis powers deserted the League, did it become more or less moribund in trying to preserve the peace. Mussolini's forces were in Ethiopia and Hitler's Germany rearmed and occupied the Rhineland, both violations of the treaties which ended World War I. Preparation for military action at a later date for the armaments industry was being developed as rapidly as possible in all three nations.

Japanese plans for future military activity increased during the early years of the 1930s, while at the same time the impatience of the younger officers in the army and navy began to cause some concern among the elder statesmen and military top commanders. It was just as it had been in the nineteenth century, when it was the younger leaders in Choshu and

Satsuma who were impatient with the leadership of the shogunate in reacting to the appearance of foreigners in their homeland. A remarkably similar series of events transpired in the early 1930s when the younger officers felt that the leadership of the older generals was unnecessarily keeping Japan from moving rapidly on the international scene. Over the course of two to three years, several assassinations of older military leaders occurred, which led the Emperor to issue an order to the military high command that this must be stopped and that the perpetrators of these acts were to be punished. Consequently, his orders were carried out, and several of the younger leaders were executed. Perhaps as a consequence of these events, the civilian government increased its censorship of numerous publications and the Japanese press.

The Japanese had been growing ever more concerned about developments in China. Since the 1911 revolution in that nation, the steady growth of Chinese nationalism continued apace. The Japanese were concerned that under the leadership of General Chiang Kai-shek, the nationalist movement would interfere with the long-term plans of Japan to form a Greater East Asia Co-Prosperity Sphere. At same time the birth of the Communist movement in China complicated the problems for the existing Chinese government, and the Japanese decided this was the time for an all-out effort to gain control of the Chinese government.

In July, 1937, the Japanese Army landed in the Shanghai area of China as the opening of its full scale operations on the Chinese mainland. They figured that the conquest of this international city would not take great effort or much time and that a quick takeover of this famous city would provide motivation for other Chinese army units to concede the issue and lay down their arms. Unfortunately for the Japanese, the rather disparate collection of Nationalist troops that were in the Shanghai area put up a desperate defense. What the Japanese thought would take them only a couple of weeks went on for several months. This proved to be a great frustration for the Japanese military leadership, so that when Shanghai eventually fell into their hands, they almost immediately decided to head for Nanking in order to prevent the Chinese from having time to regroup their forces for its defense.

The Japanese leadership was convinced that a rapid advance to capture Nanking would help erase the idea that the Japanese military would continue to have difficulty in overcoming Chinese Nationalist troops. As the Japanese Army advanced towards the city, it did not encounter any well-organized resistance. Within two weeks they had invaded the city and immediately celebrated this achievement in a manner that very rapidly got out of hand. There has never been a satisfactory explanation of the actions or lack of actions on the part of the Japanese command staff during the next few months.

The Japanese Army was completely out of control and perpetrated terrible atrocities on the civilians of all ages. Young men were rounded up and marched outside the city limits and shot so that their corpses would fall into a prepared ditch. Women were raped and then killed so that they could not tell anyone what had happened to them. Babies were grabbed from their mother's arms, thrown up in the air and caught on Japanese bayonets. This extreme cruelty and unexplainable behavior on the part of the Japanese troops has never been satisfactorily explained. I believe from everything I have read about this that the Japanese command staff wanted to set an example for other Chinese cities about what would happen if they resisted. That matters got completely out of control led to an estimated 600,000 civilian deaths in the city.

The international quarters of the city were left untouched by the celebrating Japanese troops, and when one or two newsmen and religious ministers became aware of what was transpiring, they decided that if at all possible they would record these events on film. Consequently, over the next three or four weeks they were able to obtain several reels of these horrifying events. At great risk to themselves, they decided to hide the reels on the inside lining of their overcoats and get passage to the United States.

On arrival in the United States, they had the film developed and released to *Fox Movietone News*, which ran a weekly news report on world events in most of the theaters in the United States. When these newsreels appeared on the screens of movie houses in the U.S., it created a horrifying spectacle in the public mind. While there had not been great interest shown in recent events in the Far Pacific, the Rape of Nanking caused an immediate outcry from the American public. This one event probably more than anything else led to a widespread anti-Japanese sentiment throughout the nation.

Several months before these events, an American gunboat on the Yangtze River, the *Panay*, was attacked by Japanese aircraft and sunk. There was an immediate demand from Washington that the Japanese give a full accounting of what transpired and apologize. The Japanese government issued a profound apology and explained that it was all a mistake and that the Japanese aircraft had mistaken the American gunboat as a Chinese ship.

Japan also promised to make reparations payments to atone for this obvious mistake. This was accepted by the American government, and it seemed to be a proper response by the Japanese government as far as the American public was concerned. However, more documents relating to this incident were discovered. These revealed that on the day of the *Panay* sinking, there were by chance two American newsmen in the general area of the gunboat at the time of the Japanese attack. Their film shows that six Japanese planes flying in formation at approximately 200 or 300 feet above the river level made a direct attack on the *Panay*, so that the explanation given by the Japanese authorities was totally inaccurate and the attack had been deliberate.

President Franklin Roosevelt was shown the film, and he spoke with the two newsmen who had taken the film. He asked them to remove the 40 feet showing the direct attack, saying that if the American public saw the direct attack the people would demand that we declare war on Japan. That would be a disaster, since the nation was not even remotely ready for any military conflict. The newsmen agreed to cooperate, but the American public was still upset over the incident.

The cruelty of Japanese troops to their enemies was made clear in several instances: the Bataan death march, the Rape of Nanking, and the sinking of the *Panay* were a result of average soldiers who were treated with cruelty by their own officers almost consistently. The threads of brutality and cruelty to civilians and enemy soldiers were seen in every arena overrun by Japanese soldiers.

The Japanese commander at Nanking had been chastised because it had taken his army three months to take control of Shanghai instead of two weeks, due to the totally unexpected resistance by Chinese volunteers as part of the city's defenders. And the cruelty on Bataan to American prisoners was partially a reflection of how Japanese soldiers were treated by their own officers.

When the Japanese army retreated over the mountains and jungles of Guadalcanal, the commanding officers ordered the MPs to shoot any laggards, wounded or those dying of starvation, since it would be bad for morale to see Japanese soldiers in these conditions. Guadalcanal was the first American offensive in the Pacific, in the Solomon Islands, with the intent was to gain an airfield from which our planes could protect shipping lanes from the U.S. to Australia. The airstrip, Henderson Field, was the scene of several months fighting until the area had been cleared of the enemy. The airfield was on the north side of the mountain range which straddled the island from east to west, and the Japanese had landed nearly 300,000 troops on the other side of the mountains, which rose from the jungle terrain. Our estimate of enemy casualties in the seven-month struggle for the airstrip was 25,000 killed and probably twice that many wounded enemy soldiers.

Their retreat back over the mountains and through the jungle would have been difficult at best. But Japanese troops lagging behind due to sickness or wounded were abandoned. Many fell due to starvation, and the commanders ordered their military police to shoot them since it was for morale to see some lying on the ground.

It was the usual practice that the Japanese army would live off the land and therefore little if any effort was made to ship rations to their overseas forces. I concluded that the Japanese commanders had simply written off their own troops and assumed they were no longer of any use. The best estimate was that a total of 15,000 to 20,000 survived the Guadalcanal campaign and succeeded in being picked up by Japanese coastal vessels on the other side of the island. At least half of the original Japanese troops on Guadalcanal died of disease and starvation, since the army was supposed to live off the land. The threads of this treatment have a long history in Japan's feudal past.

The Greater East Asia Co-Prosperity Sphere

For Japan, these years were ones of continuous military success as they overran all of Southeast Asia and many of the major islands of Micronesia and the South Pacific. The fall of Singapore and the destruction of British battleships were viewed by the Japanese as being proof that they were a superior military power and could almost take anything they wanted.

In this short period of time, Japan created an empire that was larger than had ever been established on this planet. It extended from Midway in the central Pacific all the way to the coast of Asia, through China and Manchuria, Borneo and Burma, and Southeast Asia and the East Indies. It expanded their empire all the way to barely 60 miles north of Australia. After they had taken some of the Aleutian Islands, their north-south territory must have exceeded 5000 miles and the east-west over 8000 miles.

This vast empire was to be incorporated into a Greater East Asia Co-Prosperity Sphere, which would have its capital in Tokyo. The Japanese plan was to use their control of this vast area as a source of raw materials and fuel, which they needed desperately, and then to develop these areas as marketplaces for Japanese industrial production.

Once the Japanese had overrun these nations, they invited the leaders to come to Tokyo for a red carpet treatment and celebration of their freedom from the domination of the white man. It made no difference to the Japanese as to what religious beliefs the people in these various nations had or if they were steadfast in their support of existing religious beliefs. This policy meant that any Christian, Moslem, Buddhist or any other established religion in any of these territories would be treated especially well. The Japanese firmly believed that all religions were conservative in nature and would therefore be more likely to accept Japanese domination rather than resort to underground counter movements against control from Tokyo.

It should be also mentioned that Japanese occupation of these areas was bitterly resented by these other cultures. I spoke with many of these adults later, and their description of the treatment they had received at the hands of Japanese troops was almost beyond belief, and their bitterness was indeed very deep-seated. In most instances, since the Japanese Army traveled without rations, the troops proceeded to seize food from the natives, who had very little to be with to begin with, and starvation or near starvation was a commonplace occurrences in many of these newly occupied areas. I remember after the war, in the 1950s, that many Japanese businessmen, who had traveled back to many of these countries hoping to reestablish their connections for trade, discovered for the first time the cruelty with which their army had occupied these areas. In the latter part of the decade of the 1950s, these businessmen wrote articles describing what had taken place in some of these cities and their profound surprise, but great dissatisfaction, with the conduct of the Japanese occupation forces.

The great success of the Japanese Army and Navy in gaining this huge new empire had to lift the spirit of the nation and strengthen its belief that the superiority of the Japanese military forces was due to the spirit and willingness of the military to fight or die for the Emperor.

Armaments

By the time that the Japanese had completely overrun this vast new empire and were anticipating exploiting it for materials and markets, the clock had almost expired and time was running out. While the Axis forces had frozen their designs in 1936 and were therefore in full production by the fall of 1939 when World War II began, the British and Americans did not freeze their designs until 1939. This meant that if they could produce later-designed weapons, their armament would be superior to what the Nazis and Japanese were using. This is exactly what transpired. If you check the timetable of World War II, you will note that, for the first three years, victories were falling to the Axis powers. In the fall of 1942, however, the reversal began to set in. The Soviet Union held fast at Stalingrad, and General von Paulus surrendered his army of 30,000 troops. The first American offensive landing took place at Guadalcanal in the fall of 1942. Rommel's troops had roamed over North Africa almost at will until they got to Egypt and were stopped by the British in the summer of 1942 at El Alamein.

From this time on, the tides of war favored the Allied offensives in the Pacific, Africa, and Eastern Front in Europe. The Battle of Midway was the great turning point in the Pacific war, since the destruction of the Japanese carriers meant that from that date forward the Japanese would be unable to carry out any offensive actions on their own. These Allied offensives continued almost without interruption until the hostilities finally ceased in 1945.

The Axis powers in Europe and the Japanese were both extremely short of fuel, and as their factories were damaged or destroyed by Allied air power, they were unable to replace their military production. The lack of metals and fuel became critical shortages for the Japanese. When the war started, the Japanese merchant marine was slightly over 12,000,000 tons and by the middle of 1945 it had been reduced to approximately 100,000 tons, made up only of small vessels which could move along the Japanese coastline.

I remember spending an evening with a Japanese prisoner whose job was to move heavy equipment. He explained to me that since the Japanese didn't have any metal to make sure batteries to defend their island empire that day confiscated any artillery pieces that they found in the lands where they had overrun. He described in great detail how Japanese had taken British Bofors down from Singapore, even with some of the concrete base left intact, and placed these on a ship for transport to the island of Truk. This would've been a distance of nearly 4000 miles and would not have been undertaken at all if the Japanese any other means of trying to defend this island.

Truk was extremely important to the Japanese since it had a 5000-foot high mountain peak in the middle and a very large reef extending all the way around the lagoon except for one small access on the western side. This truck driver explained to me how they unloaded these guns and put them on their trucks and carried him up the side of the mountain to put into the caves with guns all pointed towards the one opening in the reef through which any approaching force would have to come. He said since the mountain was high and the road obviously curved around in figure S's, that one trip from the boat with one gun would require at least two full hours of driving. He explained that frequently the trucks would break down and require almost constant repair to keep them in shape. From my own personal experience, I don't understand how the trucks could have carried a bowl for an artillery piece up any hill, let alone the ones on Truk. Many Japanese trucks had two wheels in the back and only one in the front.

Whenever I talked at length with prisoners, they were increasingly upset that they had not realized the great American industrial machine which could produce so many carriers and battleships. As the news of defeats and manpower losses from the front began to appear in the Japanese press the sense of euphoria disappeared in the grim reality of war. The

Japanese, who had been assured their homeland would always be protected, had to endure the crushing blows. After the Marianas campaigns in the summer of 1944, it became possible for B-29s to make the long trip to Japan on bombing runs and return. The distance of one of these flights was approximately 2800 to 3000 miles, and for several months the bombing runs were carried out at 30,000 feet.

General Curtis Lemay found that the altitude and the crosswinds made accurate bombing very difficult. In March, as we were engaged on Iwo Jima suffering heavy casualties, Lemay ordered his B-29s to fly in at very low levels. These first flights came in shortly after midnight, over Tokyo at first, and then over other major cities, loaded with magnesium fire sticks in large quantities. On two successive nights, March 9 and 10, the raids on Tokyo were carried out brilliantly. The planes were divided into three waves and came across the city at approximately 15-minute intervals.

The aerial reconnaissance pictures that were taken the next day after these raids were almost unbelievable. Many of the buildings in Tokyo and other Japanese cities were constructed of wood, and hence of little defense against the use of fire sticks. In the course of the next few months, the B-29s continued these raids over all large Japanese cities, with the exception of Kyoto. The ancient capital, with beautiful architecture and great historical significance and very little military importance, was exempt from these raids.

I remember talking with young children and teenagers afterwards and asked them to explain what happened when the fire raids occurred. It would be safe to say that this was a terrifying experience, and many said they were awakened in the middle of the night by their mothers and told to get out of bed because the house was on fire. When they emerged, their mother tried to get them to lay low near water, so they could avoid the flames. Their description of seeing nothing but fire all around them was quite vivid, and my guess is that these children would have these memories all their lives.

The B-29 pilots were thrilled when the battle of Iwo Jima was nearing an end and they had a field on which crippled bombers could land rather than crashing into the ocean. The crews of the crippled

B-29s that landed on Iwo were ecstatic and offered the Marines almost anything in the way of money if they had any souvenirs like an old sword or something else.

There has been a continuing discussion about the morality of bombing civilian targets. The Germans certainly carried this out in bombing London during the early years of World War II in an attempt to break the British spirit. The British used this in bombing Dresden almost into oblivion to eliminate German ball bearings production about 18 months after the raids on London. I do not know, but I think that Gen. Lemay believed firmly that, given the fierceness and intensity of the struggle on Iwo Jima, the only way to get the Japanese to surrender was to break their spirit. He ordered fire raids on several Japanese cities where there was some military production, and on others simply as a demonstration of American firepower, with the consequence that they would realize they could not win the war and agree to surrender.

7

❧

The Home Front and Wartime

Undoubtedly, throughout the decade of the 1930s, the foremost items in U.S. newspapers, radio and everyday conversation had to deal with the Great Depression rather than foreign relations. The decade following the stock market crash in 1929 was a period of intense dislocation and adjustment on the part of all Americans. Some stockbrokers simply leapt from windows on Wall Street and ended their individual struggles through suicide. Millions of others grappled with a decline in price of agricultural products that reached lows that had not existed since 1529. Millions of city dwellers lost their source of income as company after company did not adjust rapidly enough to fit the times. The unemployment rate grew steadily until it reached nearly 15% or 16%.

By 1933, when Franklin Roosevelt took office, there were more than 13 or 14 million American workers who were unemployed. It seemed that no matter what was done, everything continued to get worse. There was fear in many quarters that men who had lost their jobs and still had families to feed might resort to force to obtain what they saw as necessities of life. If five men were collected on a street corner, it was very likely that the police would come along and order them to disperse. In some cities small areas of agricultural land were made available to those living in the city so they could come out and plant their own vegetables and have something to eat.

Unemployed men roamed neighborhoods looking for jobs, many times knocking at the back door and explaining to the lady of the house that they were starving and they would do any kind of work that was necessary if the lady would please fix them something to eat.

As a boy growing up in these years, I remember some of these events very vividly, and it remained in my mind for a long time that I had seen a grown man with hat in hand and very poor clothing asking for a handout, yet being proud enough to ask to work for a little food.

When my brothers and I walked to school, our dad showed us where to walk, and on one street he was very firm in pointing out which side we were to walk on. Under no circumstances were we to look across the street where there would be men standing in line. I learned later that the men standing on the other side were in a soup kitchen line waiting to get food to take home to their families. They had their hats pulled down on the side facing the street so that they would not be recognized.

The New Deal promised to put people to work, as President Roosevelt stated in his inaugural address in March, 1933. Indeed, Congress was called into special session, and during the famous 100 days passed legislation at a dizzying pace. On occasion, Congress voted to approve legislation under only a title, with the details were filled in later by the administration. The media called the approach "alphabet soup" since there were seemingly a non-ending number of federal agencies created to handle one or another problem. The WPA, PWA, CCC, REA, TVA and countless others were created seemingly almost overnight.

The rise of the Nazi party in Germany and the installation of Adolph Hitler as chancellor in January, 1933, were hardly noticed in the American press. Most Americans paid little attention to international news, and aside from the burning of the Hindenburg in 1935 and the exploits of Jesse Owens at the 1936 Olympics in Berlin, not too much was known about what was actually happening inside the Third Reich or far-off Japan. The rise of Benito Mussolini in Italy was commented on by saying that at least he made the trains run on time. There were significant signs and events occurring in international events, but the overwhelming concern with the Depression and finding a job dominated the American scene.

A minimum wage was set at 25 cents an hour, and Saturday afternoon at the movies cost 10 cents; haircuts were 15 cents for boys under 12 and a 15 pound bag of potatoes was 29 cents. My dad and I were in a grocery store talking with the owner when a swarthy looking man ran into the store and grabbed a bag of potatoes, said something, and ran outside in a blink of an eye. My dad said, "That man was stealing, and you didn't do anything about it." The grocer replied that he recognized that man, who had three hungry children at home, and added that he had to be very desperate or he wouldn't have done this.

I knew two older boys who joined the CCC and went to camp in Colorado. They got paid 21 dollars per month, of which 16 dollars was sent home to help feed their families. Our society spawned a few gangster groups which became quite notorious, but in retrospect, as terrible as the Depression was, our society remained pretty stable, and endured. We did not know at the time, but it strengthened our resilience for the upcoming events in our lives.

The U.S. prepares

Historians still debate whether the New Deal was successful or not, but one consequence was that the federal government developed better organizations to deal with problems on a national scale. As a consequence when the situation in Europe grew ever darker in 1939 and 1940, many questions were raised about how the government could organize the economy and the daily lives of people to help the war effort. They could be answered because of our experience during the previous six or seven years.

It is almost impossible today to imagine how totally unprepared our nation was to go into combat. When the Ohio National Guard division was called up for duty and training, it was sent to Louisiana. After getting settled and starting to train, the men found that five-pound flour bags were being used as bombs and that cardboard frames were placed over small old cars, to be known as tanks. Soldiers used broomsticks as rifles, and the first guns that appeared were Springfield 1903 models, which were fine rifles in their day but would have been totally inadequate for modern warfare. There was a shortage of uniforms, and it was discovered that the old clothing from World War I was no longer adequate or even appropriate in the 1940s.

The consequences of our agreements with Great Britain about trading destroyers for 99-year leases in the Caribbean and becoming, as Franklin Roosevelt described it, the great arsenal of democracy, proved to be a great training ground for the demands that were placed on American industry after Pearl Harbor.

While our industrial base was gradually coming alive again, the situation in terms of the strength of our armed forces could not have been more serious. The size of the United States Army in 1940 was approximately 140,000 men. Most of these were garrison troops and not in any condition to enter into combat without more training. The Marine Corps had only one division that could be considered ready for action. The United States Navy was trying to recover from the consequences of the Four-, Five- and Nine-Power Pacts agreed to at the Washington Naval Conference in 1922. Part of our agreement was that we would sink or destroy some of our warships, which of course we had done.

As the war clouds became darker, and the Germans invaded Poland, there was a growing debate in our country as to whether or not we should get involved again. I doubt that any American wanted to go to war in 1940, and the first peace time Selective Service Act was passed by just one vote in the House of Representatives in September, 1940. The German Bund could meet in Madison Square Garden and attract 18,000 to hear speakers advocate isolationism as the best policy for our nation. An organization called America First included some of the outstanding leaders in our nation. Colonel Lindbergh spoke out consistently before America First groups and Senator Robert Taft was scheduled to speak to a group in Pittsburgh the afternoon of December 7, 1941.

Critics of Lindbergh reported that he had accepted a medal from the Third Reich for his contributions to aviation research and that therefore he was biased toward Germany. His views about going to war had nothing to do with that. Most people are unaware that he worked as a consultant for our Air Corps in the Pacific Ocean and made many extremely dangerous test flights of newer designs. But while the politicians were arguing over foreign policy, the great majority of Americans were cheering for Joe DiMaggio to continue his 56-game hitting streak and Ted Williams to hit 406 for the year.

The surprise attack on Pearl Harbor, led by Admiral Isuroku Yamamoto, changed the lives of every American. The "sleeping giant" that was Yamamoto's description of the United States turned out to be a most accurate one. The attack on Pearl Harbor unified the American people far beyond anyone's imagination. From radicals on the left to

Nazi sympathizers on the right and all political shades in between, the people came together as one great nation within 24 hours after the attack on Pearl Harbor. Recruiting stations were overrun with young men trying to enlist, and the armed forces were not ready to absorb so many new recruits at one time. I remember standing in the Student Center on the Ohio State University campus with about two thousand others and listening to President Roosevelt's Day of Infamy speech. I knew what I heard was important and that this would change my life.

Everything had to be done in a great rush. News from the Pacific front was consistently negative, as the Japanese empire was expanding almost at will. It invaded the Philippines within 30 days after Pearl Harbor, and in a matter of three or four months succeeded in having the remains of the American forces surrender at Corregidor. General Douglas MacArthur's promise to return to the Philippines after losing that battle was a promise for the future, which seemed to be at some distant point in time which no one wanted to estimate.

Machines for war

William Knudsen of General Motors was appointed to head up the War Production Board, which was given extraordinary powers. His performance as a "czar" was undoubtedly one of the most significant contributions in winning the war. Within the next year, America's production capacity was beginning to make a difference all over the world. Supplies of food and all kinds of military material, including jeeps and trucks, were shipped to Great Britain and through Iran to the Soviet Union, as well as Australia and New Zealand.

World War II was like no other war in a technological sense. The design of new kinds of airplanes and ships and weaponry was like nothing that had ever been seen before. The manufacture of these totally different items required that the factories be re-equipped with new machine tools in order to produce the parts for new planes, submarines, surface ships, infantry weapons and almost everything one could think of. The keys to understanding the ups and downs of World War II lay in this area of technology.

Germany froze its design of aircraft which it was going to use in

World War II in 1936. Consequently it had three years in which to manufacture the new machine tools which were going to be necessary to make the new kinds of planes and weapons that have been designed by that time. This was true all over the world, and the German invasion of Poland on September 1, 1939 was a fulfillment of the 1936 freezing of designs and German documents that reflected the status of Germany's preparations for war were clearly made by the early fall of 1937.

On the other end, Great Britain and the United States did not freeze their designs until 1939 and so logically, once these new weapons were produced, they should have been superior to those of the Axis powers. If this is true it would logically follow that the Axis powers would win from 1939 until 1942. This is precisely what happened. In nearly every corner of the earth from Africa to the Far East to the Russian front, the first three years consisted of a string of the Axis victories. The tide began to turn in 1942 with the battle of Midway in June, the first offensive action of the United States on Guadalcanal in August, and the collapse of the German army at Stalingrad in the fall of 1942 and the rebuff of Rommel's forces in North Africa at El Alamein by General Bernard Montgomery and the British Army in the same year. The year 1942 marked the high point in a string of victories for the Axis powers throughout the world, but from that time on the tide turned as American production of equipment designed with three years more planning time began to show up on many battlefronts.

What was more astounding was that under the duress of wartime needs, American scientists and engineers created hundreds of things that had never even been imagined before. Jet planes, atomic energy, hundreds of medical breakthroughs from treatment of wounds to new drugs, processes in purifying water, and countless weapons either new or totally redesigned. There were other adaptations made during battles, like the soldier who was an Iowa farm boy that suggested welding a plow on the front of a tank would help get through the hedgerows after the D-Day invasion.

The tremendous outpouring of supplies, food and machinery, as well as a remarkable array of new weapons, also had a tremendous influence on the language of the United States. There were untold new names devised for new things and differing arrangements made as to how we lived in order to get the job done. If the family had a son or father in the armed forces, it would put a blue star in the window, and of course if there were more than one member of the Armed Forces from that household, there would be more stars. If one of the members were killed, the blue star would be replaced with a gold star. There was a common term used by everyone in the United States describing the mothers of these lost sons, Gold Star mothers.

When people went to the movies and a flag was shown, there was wild cheering from the audience, and on some occasions they even rose to their feet. Wartime movies tended to glorify the actions of American pilots, sailors, soldiers and almost all sections of the military. It would not be an overstatement to say that American movie producers felt they had a patriotic duty to present movies which would be encouraging to the American public.

One of the great differences on the home front from peacetime life was devising a means to take care of shortages. We had scrap metal drives, and everyone was asked to save grease and to turn the containers in to their local butcher to be delivered to some military installations or factory for use in manufacturing. Ration books were in daily use. In every household, gasoline, shoes, sugar and meat were rationed. The ration books contained stamps which were turned in to the retail merchant when one of these items was purchased.

There were other kinds of stamps that were sold in many many schools throughout the nation. These were war stamps that were sold for 25 cents each. When a student bought one of the stamps, it was placed into a booklet so that in time the student could accumulate $18.75 worth of the stamps, when the stamp book could be turned in for a $25 war bond. There were many bond drives throughout the war, and male and female Hollywood stars participated in these drives. Many well known screen and newspaper personalities had some changes made very quickly after the attack on Pearl Harbor; the Green Hornet's faithful Japanese servant Kato became his faithful Chinese servant Kato overnight.

There was also a new government official appointed and given the name of the air raid warden. There were frequent drills, particularly in the schools and places where public activity took place, so that in the event of actual air raid people would have had some experience about what to do. Fortunately, we did not have to contend with our nation being bombed by a foreign power.

The general public reacted very strongly against anything Japanese, probably originating with the sneak attack on Pearl Harbor. I remember my dad writing me about a newspaper boy who turned a neighbor in to local police for being a saboteur. The delivery boy noted that on the porch of this house there were two chairs which had rising suns on their backs, and he thought this meant something very serious. In reality, they were simply outdoor chairs with a very colorful abstract design.

Given the great number of men and women serving in the armed forces and the great demand for additional workers in wartime factories, it was not surprising that many young people would go into the labor force. At 15 years of age, a boy could work in grocery stores and be paid 40 cents an hour. Older boys would be employed for jobs in defense plants at a wage of 70 cents an hour. There were even some high schools in the nation that divided the school day up into two parts, with Section A running from 7:30 AM until noon and then Section B from 12:15 until 4:30 PM. Students could then work while not in school.

In contrast, one seldom recognized facet of the extremes the Japanese government went to during the war concerned school children at the elementary level. The use of these children to make balloons started out as a field trip for the children one or two days a week. As the war progressed and the situation for the homeland steadily worsened, the government expanded the war effort of these children to almost five days every week. The children would report to school with a sack lunch and be transported to a large warehouse type building, where they would spend the entire day as work crews crawling all over the floor with paste and a particular kind of paper in order to make these balloons. I've seen estimates that these children made two or three million balloons in the latter part of the war. I'm not sure that these estimates are accurate, but I am convinced the process was used not only to make balloons but also to install hatred in the hearts and minds of these young people. They were told while they were making the balloons that they should chant "kill the Americans" or "kill the British." This form of indoctrination has to be one of the worst aspects of the entire war.

The tremendous string of victories for Japan from 1939 to the middle of 1942 made it appear to the Japanese that its Great Spirit of Bushido was really the key to its success. I believe that the superiority of our fighting men was at its very core based on the love of country and the freedom we enjoyed in our daily lives. This experience of living our lives as free men in the United States proved to be a stronger motivation than the abstract worship of an emperor in a nation where its culture stressed the functioning of groups of its citizens. World War II proved, at least to my satisfaction, that a society which permits freedom of choice for its citizens can become an irresistible force when there is commonality of purpose and willingness to defend the system.

Training

In our country, the selection of the young men in the U.S. who were going to go into military duty was to a great extent determined by a draft board made up of local citizens who made the final decision as to the young men that were to be drafted or exempted due to health problems or critical other situations.

In Japan, every community had an individual appointed by the government who was the official recruiter for the Armed Forces. This individual would receive orders from the government as to how many men were needed from that area. Upon receiving this order, the official would notify families that their son had been ordered up for duty and should report at a certain time in a few days. There was no appealing the decision of this official, and everyone simply obeyed the orders. Many parents privately hoped that their son would not be called but had no choice in making these decisions.

It was the usual practice that when a young man received orders to report for duty, the community would present him with a Japanese flag upon which people wrote encouraging comments around the red center of the flag. Japanese prisoners sometimes described their basic training as being a combination of extolling the virtues of dying for the emperor and learning to obey officers, no matter what commands were given.

I sensed from our conversations with parents that many considered the orders to report for service was equivalent to a death sentence, particularly after the loss of the Marianas. They thought that General Tojo's resignation meant Japan would lose the war. Most parents with whom I spoke later told me that they wished their son would not be called to military duty but that they felt there was nothing that could be done about it. I sensed from our conversations that there was a note of simple resignation in their hearts when they knew that the war was going badly.

Meanwhile, in the United States, training camps were being hastily constructed, and thousands of volunteers and draftees were putting on uniforms which did not necessarily fit individual tastes–khaki and fatigues became the attire of the day for the new enlistees. The day I went into the Marines, I weighed 165 pounds and within two weeks I was down to 149. When I finished boot camp, I was back to my original weight, but it was distributed differently and a lot more solid. I remember the quartermaster sergeant answering my complaint that I could not button my dress pants at the waist; he said not to worry because in a couple weeks I'd be able to do that–and he was right.

A little recognized aspect of training camp was the improvement in the health of the trainees. Three meals per day at almost precisely the same time, combined with vigorous exercise, created remarkable improvement in the fitness of personnel. For many, it was the best quality diet they had ever known.

One of the earliest impacts upon the new recruits came the second day, when everyone had their heads shaved and were wearing fatigues. Our drill sergeant ordered everyone to take off their helmets and look around at each other carefully. While we were observing that we were a sorry looking bunch at best, the sergeant confirmed our opinion, but added that now we all looked alike, had no money in our pockets, and would be treated exactly the same regardless of where we had come from. I saw four or five of my friends grow inches at that moment.

Many of these young men standing there had come through the Depression with very few clothes and not much food in their homes. Most of them had hopes of finding some kind of job when they had finished high school. In my graduation class of 713, only five had started to college that fall. Many had never been out of their home county in their youths, and now the entire world was yet to be discovered.

Over the next several weeks, self-confidence and a sense of teamwork were the underpinning of our training. Approximately four or five weeks later, the platoon was marching in order and becoming more and more physically fit each day. One afternoon, we were out in the boondocks supposed to be learning the four elements of a company 'on the march'. At the regular inspection the next morning, the sergeant asked the first three men in the front rank about the elements of a company on the march? Nobody could come up with them, so he asked three or four others, who likewise were ignorant, whereupon the sergeant grew more exasperated. He said to the group that if they were too lazy to learn anything the right way, he would let them learn the hard way. Following this remark, he proceeded to march the entire group out to the boondocks and conduct a close order drill for 15 or 20 minutes. There was a lot of sand, combined with high temperatures, which managed to make things miserable. The entire platoon was marching left flank, right flank, to the rear, and then repeating this over and over, so as a consequence the entire group was walking around in a whirling pile of sand, dust and dirt. Meanwhile, the sergeant in his impeccable khaki was coolly standing off to one side. Finally, after the platoon was called to order, he decided to ask the same question. This time he chose an individual who did not like his time in the corps already and was always complaining but felt that his dad, who was a state senator, would get him a discharge as soon as possible. The sergeant asked him a question, and he replied "I don't know," in such a way that meant he didn't know and that he didn't care either. This caused a wave of feeling across the entire group, and almost everyone thought even this fellow was rising in revolt. The sergeant imperturbably asked another question of one of our members, who had been a sergeant in the Army for two or three hitches and was obviously an experienced soldier. The question he put to this ex- sergeant: "What color is a grenade?" The response from the soldier was "polka dot, sir." This was again a direct challenge to the sergeant. He immediately took us back to the sandy area and we had close order drill for another 10 or 15 minutes. The difference this time was a growing volume of muttering and comments among the troops indicating that they were not going to put up with this, and added that they would get even with the sergeant one way or another.

I remember that we never did go back over the subject of a company on the march, but I do think in retrospect that the sergeant had accomplished what he set out to do: the group had come together united for a single purpose--which was to pay him back for making us march around in miserable sand and heat. In reality, it brought the members of the platoon closer together so they began to function as a unit. This was I think a very important step in the development of the fighting spirit of the Marine Corps.

Two weeks later, our platoon and about 50 others were standing on the parade ground for inspection of mess kits, which had been placed on the ground in front of each man. The officer who was the chief inspector on this occasion complemented our sergeant, saying this was the best looking group on the entire parade grounds. Nothing more was said at that time, but at mail call later that day you could hear several guys calling out to the sergeant, asking him if he could tell us again what the inspecting officer had said. Our drill instructor said he didn't pay too much attention to those kinds of things, but he was quite obviously very proud of the progress that the platoon was making.

I had dropped out of OSU to enter the service, looking for the fastest way so I could beat my brother, and the Marines were it. First, though, I had to have a bad knee fixed. I had started taking Latin in the seventh grade and kept on for four years, adding French as well in high school. I followed some advice I got from a higher up about my assignment: "Don't ask too many questions, and don't say no." Based on my school record, the Marines sent me to combat interpreters school along with 37 others, learning to read and write Japanese from Americans who had lived in the country. It was a crash course, six-and-a-half days a week, and the classroom days were 12 hours long. Only five of us finished.

We were needed. There were only 13 Americans at Pearl Harbor who spoke Japanese. Interpreters from the other services helped me learn to "live the language," especially the military words. I entered the service as a private, moved up through the ranks, and ended as a second lieutenant after the surrender.

We need to train more interpreters in this country, and in many other languages, from Danish to Farsi. You can train an interpreter for much less than the cost of a tank, and the information they can provide on other cultures and the ability to communicate is invaluable.

Life in the service

Over the next four or five years, we took full advantage of traveling at government expense for thousands of miles to places we had never heard of before. Rest bases were established in remote rear areas and became our home away from home. Living quarters consisted of six cots around the inside perimeter of our tents, which were placed about 10 to 15 feet apart along company streets. Each man had a full bucket of water under his cot for use in case of fire. At the end of each row of tents was a street where outdoor showers were located. Since there was only cold water available, I often heard remarks to the effect that if they ever got home again they never were going to shave unless they had hot water. All our worldly possessions were stored in our sea bags, which came to hold more and more as we became more adept at folding, packing and jamming things inside.

Entertainment usually consisted of watching old movies after darkness had set in. We walked a short distance with various items which we used as chairs or benches. Since our tent camps were spread out over a large area, there were eight or nine outdoor screens, which meant that one or two jeeps were used to carry the reels from one screen to another one in line, so even if all went well, it frequently happened that the projectors or the film would get tangled, and delays resulted. Sometimes it would be 15 or more minutes between reels, so there was ample opportunity for impatient audience members to offer helpful remarks to the operators, none of which were taken too kindly. A successful film splice was always greeted with loud cheers. At times a few rain showers would add to the discomfort of the troops, but these late evening shows provided some diversion for all who missed their families and loved ones back in the states.

After several rehearsals debarking from transports in the landing craft and going ashore onto a beach somewhat similar to our next invasion site, everyone loaded up his gear and we boarded the transports. I calculated that each time we went into action, we had traveled at least 3000 miles each way. Life aboard ship, therefore, consumed a lot of time. The transports usually could carry 1000 to 1100 troops and their equipment.

Our quarters were in the holds where cargo is generally carried. Each hold had metal framed beds with a canvas stretched from end to end. One side of the cot was anchored to a wall, and these were stacked about eight high with approximately two feet between each one. Such an arrangement made it difficult if you were in one of the top bunks, since you would have to crawl up over six or seven others to get to your own.

There were steel plates across the top of the canvas hold cover, on top of which landing craft were loaded. Since everything was blacked out at sea, it made it difficult to get fresh air down in the holds. Sleeping was fitful at best, and many spent a good part of the night topside.

Many would lie down on the top surface of the hold, underneath the landing craft, which was against the rules. Usually the Naval Officer of the Day, with a couple of enlisted men, would check to see if anyone was sleeping in forbidden areas. The officer and his aides were sure to make sufficient noise that when they would crawl over the hatch under the landing craft, everyone would have moved aside so that the inspection could take place. This was a successful arrangement for all.

The convoys always zigzagged across the ocean, which made the voyages even longer. Days at sea were not always difficult, since the food going into combat was satisfactory, and despite daily calisthenics there was time to write home and read books when they were available. At night you could witness spectacular astral displays from a totally blacked out environment. The skies were lit up with seemingly millions of stars, and, as our platform was constantly moving, the panorama was always different. The only news available came over a loudspeaker once or twice a day. I was quite surprised that a major topic of conversation was the European war. I guess we all knew that the main efforts of the Allied governments were to defeat Hitler's Germany. When news came of the Normandy landing, there were loud cheers, and every major advance thereafter was a boost in the morale of everyone aboard.

The seemingly unending days at sea came to an abrupt change when the convoy arrived within two days of the landing. The mood aboard ship became quieter, and time was spent cleaning weapons and checking everything that we would be carrying ashore. Briefing sessions were almost continuous on various parts of the deck, and we had our first look at the island and our intended landing areas. There were many discussions about beach conditions and specific assignments for everyone as to regrouping on land if necessary. The immediate chore once ashore was to achieve the 0-1 line that had been set as a goal by the end of the first day.

Many wrote letters to their families as the tension increased. Nothing much was said, but the arrival of flies from the island meant the convoy was nearing its goal. I noticed many of the Marines sitting and relaxing on deck reacted swiftly enough to catch flies that had landed on their arms or clothing.

D-day morning began at 4:30 AM with a larger than usual breakfast served amid rumors that our ship had passed over an enemy sub during the night but nothing had happened. This was seen as a good sign, since if our ship had been torpedoed, we would all have been dead by now. Therefore this was going to be our lucky day. By 6:00 AM the first wave and second wave had climbed into the landing craft to engage the enemy, whose background and training had been quite different.

The Japanese armed forces had been at war since July, 1937, when they had launched an invasion of mainland China. Japan had previously signed an agreement with Hitler's Third Reich and was classified as a member of the Axis powers in World War II. After the outbreak of World War II in Europe on September 1, 1939, and the subsequent collapse of France and the Low Countries in the spring of 1940, the Japanese Army worked swiftly to regain their colonial possessions in Southeast Asia.

After the sneak attack on Pearl Harbor in December, 1941, the Japanese military attacked the Philippines, Guam and Wake Island as well as other islands in the Pacific, both north and south of the equator and all the islands in Indonesia and Micronesia in the southwestern Pacific. In short order, they had expanded their empire from only 60 miles north of the Australian border to the Aleutian Islands nearly 4000 miles in north-south directions and from Midway Island in the Pacific just west of Pearl Harbor all the way into Burma on the mainland of Asia. It represented the largest empire of any one nation in the history of the world. Their string of victories and conquests was continuous for the next two years. A Greater East Asia Co-Prosperity Sphere was set up in Tokyo to control the vast new empire, which exceeded 2.5 million square miles of the earth's surface. At this point, Japanese morale, both military and civilian was at its peak. They firmly believed that their united loyalty coupled with discipline and work ethic would lead to final victory.

Japanese troops were poorly equipped to fight another industrial nation, since the critical shortage of needed resources grew steadily worse as the war continued. Their helmets were often of small size and thickness equal to about one third of ours. Their rations in the field consisted of a bag of rice, and it was expected that Japanese troops would live off the land as they invaded other nations

The Japanese infantry had well-made rifles and machine guns, in the use of which they were well trained. Artillery was another matter. I believe the shortage of metals clearly limited the production of land-based guns. One captured noncom on Iwo Jima thought we were immediately going to invade his homeland as soon as the fighting stopped on Iwo. He was also convinced that we would kill him shortly, but he asked me if I could show him our automatic artillery since he had never heard so much firepower being used at the same time. He was similarly amazed that we were not going to shoot him but transfer him down to a ship where he would go to a camp on one of the islands and sit out the rest of the war.

8

LEADERS

Admiral Chester W. Nimitz

One of the constant concerns in the Pacific arena was its vastness, which led to a division of authority at the headquarters of Admiral Chester W. Nimitz in the Navy yard in Honolulu. His headquarters was known as *CINCPAC*, which stood for the Commander in Chief Pacific Theater. Not too far away from its location was another organization solely concerned with communication, *FRUPAC*, which stood for Fleet Radio Unit Pacific Theater.

When Admiral Nimitz walked across the Navy yards, he had one Marine approximately 10 yards in front of him and another the same distance behind. I received the distinct impression from watching this that the admiral didn't want to be disturbed or interrupted in whatever he was thinking about at the time. One of his favorite stories about how the war was won had to do with a stroll he was taking on the island of Namur in the Marshall Islands. It was a very warm day, and the admiral was wearing khakis with sleeves rolled up, walking along the beach and surveying the damage and results of the battle. While he was so engaged, a front loader roared up with a big Seabee driver with no shirt on and stopped and yelled, "Hey, Mac! Where in the hell is the ammo dump?" at Admiral Nimitz. He was so taken aback by this that he just stood there saying nothing. The enlisted man with the front loader full of ammunition said "Aw, hell, this looks like a good spot," put the ammo down, posted a wooden sign saying "Ammo Dump" and roared off to get another load. Nimitz commented that this is how the war was won: an American saw a problem, made a decision, and got the job done.

The Joint Intelligence Center of the Pacific Ocean Area, *JICPOA*, was headed by an Army major named Anderson. The staff of the Center had personnel from all branches of the service who worked diligently amassing information which would be of great value in future operations. I know on some occasions they had Australian and New Zealand fishermen who had frequented some of the island areas before the war on their fishing trips. Some of them had clear ideas and notes on the movement of tides and the depth of waters around many of the islands.

In addition, combat units would assemble the latest Japanese equipment and types of weapons found in many of the island for our experts to review, so the latest information to units assigned to upcoming operations. We found that artillery and mortar officers were skilled at identifying anything that was new being used by the Japanese and getting it delivered back to the experts at the joint intelligence center. Admiral Nimitz always wanted to be notified of any and all significant weapon changes by the Japanese. He would then study these carefully and if adjustments were needed, he notified his staff to alert all necessary units.

It was *FRUPAC's* responsibility to communicate with all American ships and submarines throughout the entire Pacific Ocean area. This communication was always in code, so that the fewer symbols used in transmitting naval orders, the safer was the information sent. In contrast with our approach to transmitting coded messages, the Japanese naval headquarters, located in the Tokyo area, would frequently use historical passages or somewhat flowery language as part of their coded messages. It was this tendency which permitted our nation to solve the Japanese code, a distinct advantage to our operations. There have been many arguments as to by whom and where and how the Japanese naval code was broken by the Armed Forces. Whether it occurred in Washington DC or in the labs of the intelligence centers in the Pearl Harbor area is now just a topic for discussion.

It was my understanding that one of the code experts who was working on solving the Japanese naval code had a phrase stating that on a certain date, the third battle fleet would proceed from point A to point B. He noticed that there was a repetition of certain phonetic sounds that might be a basis to break the code. The name of the Sun goddess who allegedly came down from the mists and created the islands of Japan, spelled phonetically was O me ka me A me Te ra su. Japanese is a syllabic language, and the syllable me appears three times in a nine-syllable word. This is a rather rare occurrence that was noticed by one of the experts working on the problem. A group got together and tried various combinations and using the name of the sun goddess was the one that worked in decoding Tokyo's radio messages. This provided the information on Japanese battle plans for Midway which led to this crucial victory for our naval forces.

Yamamoto Isoroku

One of the most interesting individuals in the Japanese military establishment was Yamamoto Isoroku. He was born April 4, 1884, into a middle-ranked samurai family as Takane Sadayoshi. When he was 16, he was adopted by a well-to-do family that needed to have a son. He had shown great promise in learning and ability even in his early years.

Following his years in the Naval Academy, he received a commission and began a career which was most unusual. He had started out as a naval cadet in 1904 and over a period of 25 to 30 years worked his way up through the ranks to become the top ranked naval officer in the Japanese Navy. He had begun his career in the field of naval gunnery but changed his interests and decided to go into naval air force fields. During the great battle at Tsushima, he lost two fingers but rarely referred to this.

He attended Harvard University from 1919-1921, and followed that by being appointed to the Japanese Embassy in the United States as a naval attaché. He had become a strong advocate of naval airpower, and worked to sell its importance to his superiors. During that time, he served his nation on the mission that was determining naval ratios, which resulted in the London Naval Conference of 1930. He remained in Washington DC for another two years before returning to Japan.

He was opposed to the invasion of Manchuria following the Mukden incident and continued his opposition to Japanese expansionist plans in the 1930s. He personally visited the American ambassador, Joseph Grew, and apologized for the sinking of the US gunboat, Panay, in 1937. This meant that the attack on the USS Panay was made without his knowledge. He felt that the invasion of China was a mistake and that his nation was over extending itself without sufficient thought and preplanning.

At this time, there were more rumors that he had been designated as a possible victim of assassination attempts. The extreme right wing cadre of the Japanese military forces did not brook well his writings and announcements about his opposition to the efforts and expansion of Japanese military operations during the 1930s. When advised of these threats, he stated that he would consider it an honor to die in the service of his Emperor and paid little attention to them.

It is interesting to note that the 1932 naval planning war games in the Pacific by the Naval high command in the United States presupposed an attack on Pearl Harbor which would come from the northern Pacific. The idea behind the planning was of course that there might be an attack from communist Russia some time later in that decade. It was during this period that Yamamoto was in our nation's capital, and he obviously learned many of the details s through association with our naval personnel working on these war games.

Upon his return home in 1932, he steadfastly fought for increasing Japanese naval air power and developed tactics and specialized training ideas for Japanese pilots to learn how to fly from carriers. He was instrumental in increasing appropriations for Japanese carrier construction and training additional pilots. As a naval officer who had been educated in the United States and lived in our country for at least four years he was keenly aware of the vast industrial power and almost limitless resources available to the American government in the event of war.

He clearly understood that if Japan were to enter a struggle with foreign powers in order to gain its rightful place in Asia that it would have to win with relative rapidity should the United States itself enter the conflict. The outbreak of World War II in 1939 resulted in the fall of France and other European powers that had colonies in Asia and the South Pacific. While he was violently opposed to having his nation join Germany and Italy as a member of the Axis Powers, he saw the opportunity to gain areas containing the raw materials so vital to Japan's industrial growth. The Japanese Army and Air Force were quick to utilize the opportunities presented to them with the fall of France and the Low Countries in Western Europe to the Nazi steamroller. They quickly overran Southeast Asia and moved to within 60 miles of the northern coast of Australia as they overran the East Indies and the entire southeastern Pacific area. Their military leaders felt they would have to establish bases and defend these areas against possible action by the United States Navy. They planned on building a strong defensive cordon in the western Pacific and gradually wearing down the American forces so that they could have a negotiated peace.

It was Yamamoto's thinking that it would be very difficult to sustain defensive positions against the United States Navy so long as the Americans had aircraft carriers which could continually raid any preset Japanese defenses. He devised a plan that was totally surprising to his colleagues which centered on the idea of a quick strike against the American Navy at Pearl Harbor so as to neutralize American strength in the Pacific. He argued with other commanders and the political leadership of Japan for nearly 18 months to convince them that a carefully laid out plan could succeed in destroying much of America's naval strength in the Pacific. This would also create additional areas where Japanese expansion could occur much more rapidly and easily. After his overall strategy was finally adopted by his peers he set out to develop a plan of attack on Pearl Harbor.

The attack itself was to consist of three waves of his carrier planes which would have a defensive line between his carriers and the American bases in the Hawaiian Islands. The attack itself was a well-planned success but in his mind the failure to get off the third wave from his carriers resulted in somewhat limiting the destruction of American warships. Yamamoto was convinced that any attack on American forces in the Pacific if successful would probably provide a window of six to eight months in which the Japanese could expand in any direction without much opposition from the United States.

This assumption proved to be absolutely accurate. Consequently he decided that a strike against Midway Island which could destroy or at least further damage American carriers would probably convince the United States that it should consider a negotiated peace in the Pacific, especially being occupied with the war in Europe. The great battle of Midway in early June, 1942 resulted in an overwhelming defeat for the Japanese since the American intelligence community had deciphered the Japanese naval code. Admiral Chester Nimitz and his other commanders were well advised as to the disposition and planning of the Japanese carrier and battle fleets.

The consequences of this battle made it impossible for the Japanese to carry out any more offensive naval actions until they could repair and produce more carriers. This placed them on a defensive stance which Yamamoto set out to strengthen in the Pacific. He was on one such mission in the Solomon Islands when his plane was shot down and he was killed in April, 1943.

It was another coded message about to the plan of Admiral Yamamoto to visit near Rabaul to check on the defensive system that led to his death. The intercepted message gave the details as to the time and date that Admiral Yamamoto was to leave from Truk Island and proceed at a such and such a speed, direction and altitude arriving at his destination shortly after lunch. The message was also sent to Rabaul so that proper arrangements could be made before the admiral arrived.

There were to be also three fighter planes flying behind the admiral's for security. After the contents of the message were made known to Admiral Nimitz, he ordered that the possibility of intercepting Yamamoto's aircraft be investigated. It was decided that we had a chance, by stripping three P-38s so they could carry extra fuel which could be dropped before they arrived at point X. That point was calculated to be the center of a letter X formed by crossing the flight plan for Yamamoto going from northeast to southwest and that of the P-38s going from southeast to northwest. The P-38s would have approximately a 10-minute window in which the paths of the two airplanes would cross at the center of X.

Admiral Nimitz discussed the possibility with the Chief of Staff in Washington, George Marshall. After reviewing the pros and cons of making the attempt, General Marshall went to see President Roosevelt for final approval. Marshall reported that after he had explained in some detail the plan to intercept and shoot down Yamamoto's aircraft, the president asked him if he thought there was a good chance of bringing this plan to fruition. Marshall replied in the affirmative, and he said the president didn't hesitate and said go ahead.

In order to camouflage the fact that we must have cracked the Japanese naval code, rumors were planted with natives and civilians in several different areas of the Pacific that there seemed to be a lot of activity at air bases all over the Pacific, as if some major invasion was about to occur. It was believed that the Japanese would pick up these rumors and not deduce their code had been broken.

The P-38s encountered Yamamoto's plane, with his escorts, after three minutes into the calculated 10-minute window. The P 38s shot down the three Japanese escort planes and then Yamamoto's. They had calculated correctly, dumped the extra fuel containers and successfully returned to base.

The Japanese immediately started a search and found Yamamoto's body on a small island next to his plane. According to Japanese custom his body was cremated and one half of the ashes was placed in an urn and buried where they found his body. The other half was placed in an urn and held until the arrival of the Mitsui cruiser which had been ordered by the Emperor to bring his ashes back to Tokyo where there would be a national day commemorating Yamamoto's life.

The Japanese did not change their code at that time, and later modifications were very limited. The information about the status of the Japanese naval code was a taboo subject until after the war ended. I know that within a few days of our landing and moving across the southern part of Saipan that a crew of specialists came ashore with boxes of equipment and within three days had erected a metal tower to intercept all messages from Japanese Naval Headquarters. This was a major step in having a steady reliable signal intercept station for getting coded communications out of Tokyo. It was my understanding that Japanese Naval Intelligence never changed the code through the end of the war. This would be an unusual procedure in most nations, but perhaps the Japanese felt that the difficulties presented by their language would serve to maintain the security of the code.

Evans Fordyce Carlson

I think Colonel Carlson was the greatest man I ever knew. I first met Colonel Carlson when he addressed the top brass of the Fourth Marine division just before it was departing from San Diego. Nearly all commanders who were on the West Coast attended the session. Everyone was wearing dress uniforms, and it was a very formal occasion, with General Holland Smith speaking for the Marines on the preparations for the upcoming invasion of the Kwajalein Islands. There was serious concern that the mistakes made at the landing on Tarawa should not be repeated in the next landings. The naval representatives assured everyone that the experience would not be repeated, all of which reassurance seemed to be expected by an audience that listened politely but with a somewhat bored air.

The final speaker that night was Colonel Carlson, who came dressed in well-worn khakis and rather dusty boondockers on his feet. He did not present himself to impress anyone, and he simply began talking about the enemy soldiers and their actual battlefield strategy. His three years' experience as an observer on the Chinese Long March in the 1930s had given him an in-depth look at Japanese battle tactics. Within three minutes, one could hear a pin drop as this unassuming Marine continued to talk for approximately 30 minutes. I heard references made to his comments for several months thereafter.

Several weeks later, during the Kwajalein operation, we found some documents indicating that Eniwetok Atoll was only lightly defended and that it would be a great anchorage for staging other steps along the path to Tokyo.

Consequently, a plan was drawn up and implemented to put together some Army troops and Marine units to carry out the invasion. The actual landing occurred on February 22, just three weeks after having finished the assault on Kwajalein. The actual landing went well at first, but then the army became bogged down.

At this juncture Col. Carlson advised the Marine units to divide their front line into two lines. He directed the front group to move forward at a slow pace and to look directly ahead and around that at eye level as they progressed. He directed the second line not to look up but only look down at the ground and to shoot anything that moved.

Carlson explained that the Japanese troops were using spider traps as a means of defense. They'd dug holes, put a soldier in each, and covered it over so that it was well camouflaged. When the front-line moved across this area, the hidden soldiers would rise up behind our front line and shoot our men in the back. That's exactly what they had been doing to get the army units bogged down. Carlson emphasized again that the second line concentrate solely on looking down consistently and shooting anything that moved. This worked wonders, the adjustment solved the problem, and the island was secured within the next two hours. Needless to say, his advice saved lives.

The next time I saw Col. Carlson was on the beach at Saipan. He had just come ashore, carrying his poncho very casually, and told everyone in a very calm voice we should move inland about 100 yards. He said the Japanese artillery was zeroed in on the beach and would not make any adjustments, so by us going inland, they would be shooting over our heads. His calmness in battle was a great asset to all who were near him. It was only later that day he said that if the Germans had been defending the island, they would have adjusted their artillery pieces so that our front lines would have been under continuous fire and that would make things much more difficult.

About two weeks later, he suffered a severe wound and was taken to an aid station from which the wounded could be placed on a hospital Jeep for transfer to the beach and then to the hospital ship off shore. When the next Jeep arrived, Col. Carlson declined to go before a corporal who had been there first in line at the aid station. Carlson's actions always spoke louder than any words.

He had already studied the island of Tinian, just three miles south of Saipan, and devised a landing plan that was most unusual. We followed his plan in every detail when we landed on Tinian and found that it made its conquest much quicker and the loss of life much less. On the hospital ship, his wounds were attended to, and I visited him later in the Aiea hospital. His thoughtfulness and concern for all Marines made him one of the most admired officers in the entire Corps. He lived in southern California after the war and died in 1947. Those Marines that came in contact with him will always remember the things in life for which he stood.

9

TALES OF THE MID-PACIFIC

Tom Thumb the Train

Probably the busiest area in the entire Pacific Ocean during World War II was the island of Oahu. In addition to the city of Honolulu and the numerous naval, army, air, and coastal defense units, there was of course the Naval Headquarters, where military personnel moved in and out for many varied reasons. Most of these were wounded men released from the hospital and waiting for transportation to return to their former outfits. This might entail waiting for one or two weeks before one could be returned to his outfit, which could be located almost anywhere in the vast regions of the earth's largest body of water.

During the waiting period, the tent camp in the Aiea area became a temporary home. Upon arrival, one would go to the quartermaster supply area and be issued a mattress, linens, and directions to a tent somewhere on the base. Once there and unpacked, the newcomer knew absolutely nobody, and so he would find a one- or two-week veteran of Aiea and inquire as to the major issues of the day: Where was the local slopshute, or beer joint, what did you need to go on liberty, and where was the mess hall? Once you knew, there was nothing much to do and no buddies around with whom you could pass the time of day; so you looked for an easy way to get to downtown Honolulu, a dozen or so miles away. Being alone in a crowd of thousands of strangers brought thoughts of home into many minds.

It was about this time that you would hear a train whistle from an old steam locomotive. Tom Thumb was starting one of its daily trips from the Navy yards to downtown Honolulu. The small size of the engine made no difference to anyone, and the passenger cars were swamped with service men of all branches. I think the fare for a ticket, which one bought from the conductor, was 25 cents. The windows were all open and provided easy access for men running to get aboard. I think that Tom Thumb had a top speed of 10 miles per hour, so as it chugged along large numbers of men climbed aboard through windows with help from those already on board. In five or 10 minutes Tom was overloaded with riders, and the aisles were jammed with standees. The conductor, who wore the traditional uniform as in the states, adjusted to this without any concern and quite frankly seemed to enjoy the popularity of his train. Obviously, he could never get from the rear of the train to the front to collect fares, but he just laughed all the time, enjoying appreciative comments from homesick service men who reveled in this reminder of trains in the states.

So Tom Thumb chugged along at its leisurely pace and tootled his whistle, knowing how much it was appreciated by all. He probably brought some cheer into the hearts of thousands who were thousands of miles from home.

Master Sergeant Abie Collins

One of the most interesting Marines I met in the entire war was Master Sergeant Abie Collins. He had been in the Corps for so long that he had service stripes up both his sleeves. He must have had 10 hitches before Pearl Harbor. He was almost as far around as he was tall in the 1940s. During World War II, he was the main chef for the headquarters company of the Fourth Division. His voice was slightly below a dead roar, and his biceps were indicative of great physical strength. His life had been committed to service in the Marine Corps. In many ways, Abie was his own boss, and yet everyone benefitted from his long years of preparing food under all kinds of battle conditions. I remember that on Saipan he had his chefs, about a dozen, unload all the mobile gear from the ships and take it ashore by the end of the second day. On the third they were delivering fresh hot bread to troops in the forward areas.

When the Seabees came ashore about the ninth or tenth day of the battle, Abie was right there to get a kitchen constructed in less than 24 hours and feed both the Seabees and the Marines in the southern part of the island.

When the division returned to its rest base on Maui after the Marshalls campaign, to everyone's dismay there had been nothing constructed except for the divisional headquarters. Somehow, Abie managed to get the wheels moving in his direction, and a large mess hall was soon under construction. This building was situated on a hillside, so that after the troops had gone through the chow line, they had to walk over to the large tent where they would eat their meals. Since it had rained overnight, the slippery slope caused many to fall and lose their food. There were no other mess halls operating in the entire camp, so very shortly the chow line had a thousand or more men from all over the division standing in line waiting to eat. Abie and his cooks worked continuously to serve hot meals right up to 11:00 PM that night.

When the assistant divisional commander came by to see why the chow line was so long and taking so much time, Abie proceeded to point out in very loud and implicit terms the difficult conditions. Some of the troops shouted encouragement at Abie to tell the general what was going on, although the sergeant did not need any advice.

Several weeks later, the division brass decided it would help morale if they set up contests among the mess halls scattered around the rest camp. Each of the nine battalions and the special weapons company and artillery units had their own mess halls. Every Monday morning, the winning mess hall was given an award pennant which would be raised in front of that mess hall. It seemed that many of the battalion mess halls were always getting the award, and Abie's groups failed week after week. Nothing was said about this seeming discrimination by the judges.

In the tenth week of the contest, the 3rd Battalion, 25th regiment got the award, even though it was on maneuvers and the only food served was boxed C rations. Abie was furious about this, and the next Monday, when he saw the award flag flying in front of his mess hall, he decided to take action.

He ordered all his cooks to form two lines and march up to the divisional command headquarters center. He had two drummers and a bugler accompany them as they marched up the hill and stood at attention before the flag pole in front of the commanding general's area. Abie had two of his chefs raise the award pennant up the flag pole with a roll of the drums and the bugler sounding the charge. The sergeant then saluted and marched his crew back down the hill.

The commanding general was Clifton Cates, who had just assumed command about 10 days prior to this. He recognized the humor of this and did nothing. Everyone thought this was a good sign. The next week he learned that the troops, although they were combat veterans, were still being given training. General Cates then issued an order to cut off the training and let the troops rest or engage in sports. This made him all the more popular. He later became Commandant of the Marine Corps.

When the division returned to camp after the Marianas campaign, which had lasted all summer, Abie looked around to see if he could improve the quality of food. He discovered that the Army had a warehouse on the island and that its inventory was vastly superior to that which the Marines had.

He thereupon decided to take action and correct the disparity. He knew the night time sentries would be new, since guarding a locked warehouse did not require much in the way of protection. On the appointed evening, he assembled about 10 of his chefs and two six-by-six trucks and took off for the warehouse, which was in a somewhat secluded area.

Upon arrival Abie jumped out of one truck and commenced shouting orders to back up to the big overhead doors of the warehouse. When the young sentry appeared and asked what was happening, Abie waved a fistful of some official-looking orders and yelled at the sentry to get out of the way. He had his orders and if someone had forgot to inform the sentry, that was not Abie's problem, so just get those doors open and get out of the way. The sentry was overawed by this tough roaring master sergeant and did as requested.

Abie never ceased shouting orders about what boxes to get and load onto the trucks and waving his fake orders in the air. The whole operation took about 25 minutes. With the two trucks now loaded up, they took off, with Abie telling the sentry to be sure and lock the doors and how he would not complain to his superiors that someone had forgot to properly inform the sentry. Abie had figured out that the next warehouse inventory was not scheduled for three weeks, by which time all the evidence would have been consumed.

On another occasion, there was a company formation ordered for

7:00 PM to hear the rules and regulations of the Corps, known as the Rocks and Shoals of the Marines, and nobody liked to hear them. Abie realized that the officer had had the company line up in a 'company front' formation rather than in columns, and that hence, when the officer started to read the regulations, those standing more than 50 feet to either side could not hear. Since Abie was one of these, he raised his voice and shouted that the men around him could not hear. Consequently, the officer raised his voice considerably. Abie repeatedly yelled that he still could not hear. In a few minutes, the chords on the officer's neck were standing out as he was now practically yelling at the top of his lungs. After another few minutes the meeting was ended, and at this point Abie casually walked up to the officer and said quite loudly that there was no reason for the officer to yell at the troops. I doubt that the officer, who was new to his assignment, fully understood that Abie had been baiting him for most of the session.

He was equally adept in being ahead of everyone else when getting things set up at rest base when returning from combat. I recall getting back to port about 8:00 PM, with a steady rain on Maui. The unloading of equipment of all kinds started about 9:00 PM, and this entailed loading the nets on the decks of our ship with our gear and then depositing it on the docks, from where it was reloaded onto trucks for the long haul back to the rest base. Somehow, Abie got several trucks arriving from camp right on time, and his cooks and chefs loaded their stuff in the trucks and disappeared into the night. They opened the mess hall and started serving breakfast by 3:00 AM in the morning. Abie's crews continued serving without stopping until 6:00 PM the following afternoon. It was the only mess hall open in the entire division.

Everyone else spent the entire night in the rain unloading our gear and reloading it onto the six-by-six trucks, which had canvas covers. It was quite chilly, and everyone was really tired when a small truck drove onto the dock and stopped. Two middle-aged men and two women got out and immediately opened up the sides of the truck on one side and started making donuts and hot coffee. It was the Salvation Army at work, and everyone cheered. Everyone's mood was lifted up by their appearance. They served the Marines until 6:00 in the morning when the last truck pulled out headed up to the camp.

In talking with these Salvation Army personnel, they told us they had signed up for five full years overseas without any leave, which we found very impressive. The service they rendered that night on a small island and without headlines or any notice was deeply appreciated, and they made a lot of friends for their organization.

Truk Island

The central Pacific was where the first invasion of Japanese-held islands occurred in 1943. The first of these was Tarawa, where the landing was jeopardized by the misreading of the tides, which contributed to heavier causalities. The second landing was on January 31, 1944, with a subsequently assault on Eniwetok on February 22. While our next main goal was to attack the Marianas Islands, Truk Island was an important non-battle in the strategy of the Pacific war.

The island called Truk was located 7 degrees north of the equator and had a large harbor with a large reef extending for more than 140 miles around the outer limits of the islands which made up the Truk group. The harbor itself encompassed an area of 820 square miles. The 11 varied size islands which made up the group added up to just under a total land area of 50 square miles.

Truk was called the Gibraltar of the Pacific, since it was used as the staging area for all the Japanese naval activities south of the equator, which included all of the Solomon Islands. Given its immense size and the large lagoon, it became possible for the Japanese to practically put their entire Navy into this one area.

The island was originally Spanish, and after the Spanish-American War in 1898 the Germans took control of the island and held it until the end of World War I, when it was placed under the mandate authority of Japan by the League of Nations. The true name of Truk was Chuuk, which was the name of one of the native tribes that first came into the area, probably about 1000 years before. Truk itself as a name was a mispronunciation of the original name for the area. There was not only a large portion of the Japanese fleet in the lagoon many times there were also naval shops and storage facilities for various kinds of naval parts and supplies.

In early February, 1944, the Japanese had battleships, carriers, cruisers, destroyers, tankers and cargo ships and even minesweepers anchored in the great lagoon at Truk. When the decision was made early in February that we should make a leapfrog to Eniwetok, which was 350 miles west of the Kwajalein Atoll, a further decision had been made about what should be done with the harbor at Truk. The result of these deliberations was that Task Force 58 under Admiral Marc Mitscher would be given the responsibility for neutralizing the Japanese fleet in the lagoon area. Task Force 58 went into action on February 16 and 17 and spent three days destroying anything that would float and all of the Japanese supply centers and machine shops. The big Japanese battleships left the lagoon just in time to avoid the carrier air attack, but Admiral Mitscher's force destroyed 12 other warships, 32 merchant ships and 249 aircraft.

I was somewhat suspicious of the numbers that were given for this battle, but the visible remains of all these sunken vessels are still visible in the lagoon and harbor area today. It has become a frequent vacation spot for deep-sea divers with cameras to take pictures of various Japanese battle regalia and the ships which still exist.

Needless to say, this destruction over the three days eliminated Truk for anything insofar as the war was concerned. It was considered a daily milk run for the B-24 bombers to fly from Eniwetok over Truk and drop a few bombs on anything they thought was worthwhile. The action by Task Force 58 simply opened the way for a clear uninterrupted path to the Marianas.

Until the war ended, the entire Truk area was totally isolated and cut off from receiving any food or supplies of any kind for the entire period. As a consequence, it was estimated that approximately 2000 of the natives had died of starvation. The capture of the island was probably the best and by far the easiest of the entire war.

Two months after the surrender was signed in Tokyo Bay, an American medical doctor went ashore and received the official surrender of the entire area. From the years since that event till shortly after the start of the twenty-first century, Truk was the responsibility of the United States under the United Nations. In that time, we made considerable progress in the hygiene and health of the natives as well as improved living conditions and education. The area can now be reached by regularly scheduled airlines, and the attraction of underwater camera work has brought frequent visitors to the area. '

Tokyo Rose

One of the most popular radio broadcasters from Japan during World War II was a person named Tokyo Rose. In all actuality there was never any one person who functioned as this alleged Tokyo Rose. The name was made up by servicemen in the Southwest Pacific area who could listen to this female voice over Radio Tokyo every night around midnight. There has been much discussion and research about who this person was, and there has never been total agreement.

The best information available seems to indicate that no fewer than six or seven different English-speaking women acted as commentators on the American musical program which emanated from Tokyo, usually at midnight. The female voice issued a warning to American servicemen about the great troubles they were in and said they were losing the war and it would just be a matter of time before the Japanese Army and Navy overran their positions. This propaganda continued on and off as parts of the broadcast for three or four years.

Much of the information that was given was clearly propaganda, although allegedly she would mention servicemen by the name and the outfit to which they belonged, which seemed to attract some attention.

After repeated research by our government and several news teams, the general consensus was that Iva Toguri, in all likelihood, was the person identified as Tokyo Rose. Toguri had been born in the United States and could not speak Japanese at the time of Pearl Harbor. She had gone to Japan to visit relatives, and there met a young man she married. He apparently was having serious health problems, and she worked as a typist in the studios of Radio Tokyo.

There was already another person who was doing these broadcasts, and Iva had done the typing and some of the writing for these programs. After some months, the lady who was doing the broadcasts fell ill, and so Japanese authorities asked Toguri to take her place. Toguri testified later that she had done some broadcasts but denied she had ever said anything that would be damaging to the morale of American Army and Navy personnel.

In 1951 she was formally charged with broadcasts detrimental to the security of the United States. She was finally convicted of this charge and had great difficulty in obtaining permission to come back into the United States, even though she was an American citizen. Her husband had died of his physical problems, and she struggled to have her name cleared. Finally during President Ford's administration, the matter was reviewed again and he issued a full pardon.

There was never anyone else charged with being Tokyo Rose, and since the name had been created by American servicemen, it would be almost impossible to indicate that a voice over Radio Tokyo could have been clearly identified. There have been several movies and stories about Tokyo Rose, and I think she has become a very active part of some people's imaginations.

Kahalui

One of the nicest times that I had during the entire war was a trip from the port of Kahalui on the island of Maui to Pearl Harbor. What made the trip so nice was that it was on a small 80-ton ship that would travel about 12 knots per hour. The purpose of these trips was to deliver a collection of enemy materials that we had identified as being something different on the island of our last invasion. This meant that new kinds of ammunition or different models of weapons or special equipment would be gathered together and set on the dock of the port where our rest base was located. The next day we would load this material onto the little boat, with most of it sitting on the decks, and that evening start the trip to intelligence headquarters near Honolulu.

Since the distance was about 80 miles, it would take six or seven hours to make the trip. Our little ship usually left about 9:00 PM and arrived early the next morning. There was no need to be in a hurry, since the defensive nets that protected the entrance into Pearl Harbor would not be lifted before 6:30 or 7:00 AM. This was an exciting scene as all of the fishing boats would be racing to get in ahead of the others so they could be sure to sell their entire catch that day.

The voyage in the evening was made more enjoyable since everything was blacked out, and there were only a few dimly lit red lights on our vessel. This was the first time that I had witnessed the skies over the Pacific Ocean in total darkness. From horizon to horizon it seemed as if there were millions of stars in the heavens, which made a view of a late night sky in the states seem very paltry. The tugboat chugged along at its slow speed, making it a very peaceful scenario. I looked forward to these few trips for this very reason. The thousands of miles that all of the servicemen spent while on transports and then assault vessels, with bombardments and aerial strafing, had almost convinced us that when we got on a ship it was going to be very noisy from beginning to end. These trips were the exception.

Once our small vessel had arrived and docked in the Navy yards, we saw that all of the equipment and material aboard was taken directly to the laboratory of the joint intelligence center. The technicians who checked on the items that we brought were very thorough in their work. Whenever they discovered a different kind of ammunition or a modification of a rifle or change of any other regular equipment of the Japanese Army, it would be carefully analyzed and reported to central intelligence. After this information was reviewed, it was used to develop notification to all combat units so that the new knowledge could be incorporated into battle plans.

While this was going on, I would report to the joint intelligence center and be assigned to a prisoner of war camp. We conducted in-depth interrogations to find any new information about specific islands which we were going to assault in the near future. The silence and quietness of our overnight voyage contrasted greatly with the noise in every other aspect of our activities in the war. It made it seem as if I had been on vacation for at least a short time.

POW camps

The camps were located on spits of sand which jutted into the ocean, so they were more easily guarded. Japanese troops were never informed about the Geneva Convention, which stipulated that a prisoner had only to give his name, rank, and serial number to his captors because it was felt they would never be captured. Our strategy in talking with prisoners on the battlefield tended to follow a pattern which seemed to justify its continuation. When captured, a Japanese soldier would be convinced that we would subject him to all sorts of brutal torture and certainly put him to death sooner or later. Being taken prisoner was an awful psychological shock. The personal disgrace this would bring to a family was beyond description and meant that they were entering a period in their life for which they had absolutely no understanding or background.

What seemed to work for us was to tell the soldier immediately that as far as he was concerned "the war was over." If he were wounded, we would try to get the nearest corpsman to take a look at him and at least render first aid. Most of them had been without water and eagerly drank a lot.

We would tell them to look out at the invasion fleet and point out the hospital ship, which had a red cross on its side. We told the prisoners that they would be taken to a ship like that for further medical treatment if needed and ultimately shipped back to some small island where they could sit out the rest of the war. We also offered them some pogey bait, such as a D ration or candy bar, if we had any, and then a cigarette. These acts were done as calmly and quietly as possible as if they were simply the routine manner in which prisoners were treated.

The best cigarettes the Japanese had were Shikishimas. They were loosely rolled with very thin paper and shipped in wooden crates, which often either dried out the tobacco or made it damp from collecting moisture. In any case, when a prisoner was given an American-made smoke, he was truly very satisfied. We had off-brands of American cigarettes which left much to be desired when compared with the major name brands. We could always tell eventually how long a POW had been a prisoner when he would refuse an off-brand and ask for a Camel or Chesterfield instead.

We tried to make notes on our conversations with each prisoner as to his personal information and some details we had learned about him. We also made every effort to accurately note the places he had been since had been in the Japanese army or navy. These notes followed him all the way to the prisoner of war camp where he was assigned. When possible, we would have a second interview with the prisoner aboard a transport on the way back to where his camp was located.

These conversations took quite a different tone, since he now understood that he was not going to be killed or tortured in any way. He had already developed a taste for American cigarettes and asked if we had these in the POW camps. It was frequently the case that one of the places he had been stationed was on our list of possible invasion sites, the POWs had no hesitation talking about the area and what they did.

These discussions were of great value when combined with other information about these sites. The detailed battle plans for each invasion used much information from these sources and afforded the assault troops data which proved to be essential. All of these bits of intelligence were forwarded to the Joint Intelligence Center (JICPOA) at Pearl Harbor. This assemblage of information was of great value in the planning of future action.

As far as I could tell, the treatment afforded Japanese prisoners of war was in accordance with the Geneva Convention. At first, the food provided was the same as that in the regular troop kitchens. Shortly thereafter, several prisoners complained that they were having severe stomach disorders and asked if they could go to sick call the next morning. Their explanations as to the cause of their illness varied, but at least several of them attributed their sickness to having inhaled too much smoke during the battle before they were captured. Others thought they might have been given poisonous food or drink. I thought about the various causes they reported, but nothing seemed to make much sense.

I remember that on Saipan that Japanese soldiers would fill up their canteens with water from small streams, with dead animals and even a few corpses not more than 20 or 30 yards upstream. They carried rather large pills the size of large Brazil nuts in a small bag attached to the fundoshi around their waist. These pills turned out to be creosote, and they explained that by using these pills, they could drink any water and enjoy its natural taste. They thought our water, which had been purified, had a funny taste to it and therefore their system was better.

After a week or two of these complaints and health checks by our doctors, it was determined that the regular diet of our troops was far too rich for the Japanese, and that switching to unpolished rice and eliminating nearly all fresh fruit and juices would be all that was necessary to solve their discomfort. The diagnosis was correct, and in a matter three or four days there were no more complaints.

Bill Brown, a Navy interpreter, and I were interviewing a young soldier who had been captured on Tarawa and had just been transferred from a hospital to a prisoner of war camp. I would guess him to be 18 or 19 years of age. I think we spent a couple of hours one evening talking with him about his family and how his wounds were healing.

He decided he wanted to talk about what had happened and took off his shirt to show us. The back of his neck and shoulders showed the results of being struck with a sword several times. Thanks to sulfa, most of the wounds had closed, but the scars were permanent. He explained that he and about 12 to 15 others were inside a bunker when they saw the Americans go by them and realized that they would be captured. The officer who was in the bunker with them ordered all to face towards the Imperial Palace in Tokyo and, giving each one of them a cup of sake, ordered them to toast the emperor, apologizing for their failure to defeat the enemy.

Next, he ordered them to get down on their knees and bow their heads. He then drew his sword and proceeded to decapitate his own troops rather than have them endure the shame of being taken prisoner. Apparently, by the time the officer got near the end of the line, his weapon had become too dull or he did not have the strength to finish. We asked the prisoner what happened next, and he said he heard a shot but apparently collapsed at that point. This was completely beyond my comprehension. I read once that prewar Japan was a culture dedicated to death. It may have been an overstatement, but what that prisoner said does raise doubts.

The prisoner with sword scars on his upper back and neck seemed to be an extremely rare case. After the war, we learned that the usual policy of the Japanese High Command was simply to omit certain basic requirements of an army invading a foreign county, which frequently led to abuses of their own troops.

Another event which occurred in a prisoner camp also gave me food for thought about the needless cruelty of some Japanese officers. In accordance with the Geneva Convention on the treatment of prisoners it was necessary for us to protect them from being used as forced labor. If they were put to work, the specific conditions as to how this work was to be done were fully enumerated.

In one camp, a crew of prisoners was working on a road outside the fenced-in area with three Marine guards standing off to one side as security. It was a pleasant sunny day, and it appeared as if everything was going along fine. A Japanese officer came along and noticed one of the prisoners was not working as hard as he should. He called the prisoner to stand at attention and then proceeded to knock him to the ground with a punch to his head. The prisoner immediately jumped up and stood at attention again. This process was repeated at least five times. The officer then turned, dusted off his uniform, and strutted off. The prisoners said nothing. The three Marines laughed at this at first and then were disgusted and wanted to interfere.

San Francisco

Towards the end of April, 1945, I arrived in San Francisco for reassignment. There were diplomats from 50 nations for the signing of the documents creating the United Nations. There was an air of excitement on the streets in anticipation of the meetings and many special events scheduled. One of these was a performance by the San Francisco Symphony Orchestra in downtown San Francisco. I decided that since it had been a long time since I had gone to any serious music production, I would attend, and found myself an overcrowded auditorium. The first half of the program consisted of several pieces from around the world to honor the occasion.

The second half was to be a violin concerto with Yehudi Menuhin as the soloist, since he resided in the port city. When the second half of the concert started, a rather tall young man nonchalantly carrying a Stradivarius violin in his hand got up from a front row seat and casually walked up on stage. This was our soloist for the evening. His performance could only be described as being a virtuoso delight and drew rave applause from the audience.

Following the concert, a fellow Marine and I stopped at a local pub for a couple of drinks and shortly after midnight we ended up in a large cafeteria in order to get a cup of coffee. After about 15 minutes, three or four young people walked into the cafeteria and sat down at a table near us and started playing and singing. There were only 30 or 40 people in this vast cafeteria. Soon people from all walks of life and in all kinds of attire came in and join in songs which everyone seemed to know. After an hour or so, there were no fewer than 300 people who were sitting and singing together all of these tunes. I noticed that the delivery men who came in around three or four o'clock in the morning to deliver food and other materials for the cafeteria to use that day would stop and join in the singing.

This most unusual combination of people struck me as being part of an extraordinary event. Everyone there was a stranger to everyone else, and yet there was warmth and a sense of fellowship in which everyone participated. Finally around 6:00 AM people began to drift off, either to go to work or to go back to their lodging for some sleep.

I have seen something similar to this several times in Europe, but it always consisted of local inhabitants who clearly knew each other and did this rather often. I though afterwards that the casual and unforeseen meeting of these people from all parts of the country reflected the spirit of the American people during World War II. The genuine warmth and sense of fellowship that was apparent in that cafeteria was a manifestation of the freedom with which Americans have always taken for granted.

Such an event could never have taken place in Japanese society, which was so highly structured and socially regulated that for 200 or 300 strangers to get together and sing and enjoy themselves would be completely out of question. The mix and exchange among those Americans from all levels of society and all variety of employments and national origins continues to standout in my mind as constituting one of the great strengths of our nation.

10

SAIPAN AND TINIAN

Following the Battle of Midway, in which the Japanese carrier forces were seriously diminished, it became possible for the United States to start a drive across the central part of the Pacific Ocean towards the mainland of Japan.

The first of these landings took place at Tarawa, but unfortunately the first waves of Marines going ashore found that they were strung up on the reef since the tides were misread. This meant the Marines had to walk the remaining distance to the beach carrying their weapons over their heads and being entirely vulnerable to Japanese defensive fire. Once on the beach, it was necessary to reorganize and eventually start to push forward in some areas.

The battle lasted three days, and for most of that period fighting was very intensive. The island was secured by the fourth day, and the momentum of the drive across the central Pacific continued. It's worthy to note that at the time of the invasion of Tarawa, plans had already been made for the attack on the Kwajalein Islands and very shortly thereafter it had been determined to bypass Truk enroute to the Marianas.

The planning staffs for these operations were housed in naval headquarters in Honolulu. The unbelievable complexity of their tasks seemed only to multiply at a very rapid rate. The great distances in the Pacific Ocean were the underlying factor affecting nearly everything we did. There was a meeting on the West Coast in December, shortly after the Tarawa operation, to discuss what had gone wrong that had made the landing process very costly. The necessary corrections had been made for the Marshall Islands and the operations went smoothly and effectively.

One of the very fortunate things that happened was the discovery of some enemy documents indicating that Eniwetok was lightly defended at that time. A hastily improvised invasion force was put together, and on February 22 we landed on the island and after some difficulties with spider traps moved across the island and secured it on the same day.

In many ways this was a real bonus since the lagoon was quite large and provided a great marshaling area for the invasion of Saipan and Tinian. Of course, by this time the planning for the upcoming invasion which was scheduled for the middle of June was already far along and the necessary preparations long since underway. This meant the planning for everything that would be needed had to be reviewed and delivery times changed so that the invasion could come off on time.

The plans for the invasion included the use of ships that had not yet been built and supplies and ammunition not yet made, so that the pressure on the home front to get things done on time was steadily increasing. The great D-Day invasion in Europe was scheduled for June 6 and the Saipan landing for just eight days later.

One of the major strategic decisions made late in 1943 was that we would not invade the island if Truk, which was considered by many to be the Japanese Gibraltar in the central Pacific. The elevation of the mountains on the island and the extensive reef of over 140 miles only had one small area where ships would have access. This meant that the Japanese would have their big guns located at an elevation and zeroed in on the only area in which ships could enter. This made it necessary to neutralize Truk if at all possible. The runways on the air strip on Eniwetok were sufficient to handle the B-24 bombers that began to make regular raids on installations on Truk. In addition, Admiral Marc Mitscher and his carrier fleet were given the responsibility for eliminating anything that was afloat in the Truk harbor.

The carrier attack over two days succeeded in wiping out numerous ships and destroying naval shops and installations which had been capable of making repairs.

The lagoon at Eniwetok was the staging area for our major operation in the Marianas, with Saipan being the first landing site. Nearly every ship in the Navy, including transports, had masts that raised a considerable height above the top deck. There were so many ships in the lagoon that if you did not look down and see the water, you would think you were in a big city, since there were so many installations for communication purposes on all of the ships. There were no televisions at that time, but it simply looked like there were thousands of television antennas.

Actually the lagoon consisted of transports for two Marine divisions and one Army division. It also contained the carrier fleet Task Force 58, the battle fleet which was definitely going to be contacting the Japanese battle fleet west of Saipan, and the bombardment group under Admiral Raymond A. Spruance. In addition, there were destroyers and destroyer escorts and seemingly 200 or 300 transports carrying all kinds of supplies and goods and ammunition and a couple of oil tankers. I had never seen so many ships in my life. Pilots who were flying from the lagoon to Saipan and back, a distance of 1100 miles each way, said they were never out of sight of our naval armada and the invasion fleet. The transports had started out first since they were slower but after a couple days the fast moving battle fleets and carrier fleet's were also underway for the Marianas area.

I still have a difficult time believing it possible that our country could stage a D-Day invasion on June 6 in Europe and the Marianas invasion only eight days later. The two landing areas for these invasions were about 13,000 miles apart. The ships that were involved in these operations did not exist at the time of Pearl Harbor. The tremendous productive effort of everyone in our nation had to be involved to make these landings possible. The generation of new ideas for production and the training of millions of workers, including women who had never been in the labor force before, simply staggers the imagination to see how much could be done.

Taking the fight forward

Until the summer of 1944, all battles in the Pacific had been on islands which had not been originally the property of Japan. Japan had received all the islands north of the equator as part of the Versailles Treaty in 1919. According to the agreements reached by the League of Nations, it was improper to do anything to fortify these islands and Japan could not build any military installations on these islands. But the League inspection teams had never been able to inspect or visit any of the islands that were under Japanese control.

Many of these islands had been retaken by our forces over the past 18 months, but the struggles on some occasions were very fierce and costly. It was anticipated that when we invaded the islands that had long been the property of Japan, the struggles would last longer and be more costly.

The Marianas islands were about 1500 miles south of the Japanese mainland and consisted of four islands. The largest of these was the island of Saipan, and only three miles to the south was the island of Tinian. Between Tinian and the island of Guam was a small island called Rota, which had been used for target practice for many years and was not inhabited. The island of Guam, on the other hand, had been a territory of the United States since the Spanish-American War ended in 1898. Guam was inhabited by natives who were known as Chamoros. They had prospered under American tutelage over the first 40 years of the 20th century. The health and educational standards of the people had been vastly improved, and the population for the most part had at least a high school education equivalency.

The decision to invade the Marianas chain had been made by Admiral Nimitz's command staff in the middle of November, 1943. At that time, the battle of Tarawa had just been finished. The battle for the Marshall Islands would occur at the end of January, 1944, and all preparations for that had already been made. There was no anticipation at that time that the island of Eniwetok would be in our possession before the end of February, 1944. To further complicate matters, the planners in the nation's capital were totally involved in making preparations for the D-Day landing in Europe on June 6, 1944.

The planning groups in *CINCPAC, JICPOA* and *FRUPAC* faced an almost insurmountable task. There were questions about which troops might be ready to make the invasion. Which ships and transports would be ready or even constructed in time to handle a half million or more troops and all the supplies and equipment that would be needed to support the invasion?

There were troop carrying ships and cargo transports of approximately 18,000 tons which were being turned out by the Kaiser Shipyards in San Francisco. Under orders from President Roosevelt, the shipyards achieved unheard of efficiencies and were able to completely finish one of these transports in 30 days after the keel had been laid. This meant that the shipyards were running 24 hours a day, seven days a week, using thousands of women who had never done this kind of work before. The urgency in getting the ships produced and then having crews ready to operate them presented a real challenge for many parts of the naval service.

Once a ship was launched, it was the Navy's responsibility to have a crew ready to sail the vessel within two weeks' time. This meant that experienced naval officers would take over the ships with a very young and inexperienced crew that had only been in the Navy for a matter of two months. The training cruise would last slightly more than two weeks and took place up and down the Pacific Coast. Very shortly thereafter, the new ships and crews would be ordered overseas. I well remember landing craft being handled by young sailors who may have been 18 or 19 years of age making the run for the shore as the Marines hit the beach. They would immediately head back to their transport to get another load of either Marines or supplies.

Once a landing had taken place, the Marines ashore were probably awake for the first three days and nights of the battle. It really wasn't much different for the sailors who were involved in the operations either, handling the landing craft or unloading cargo from the transports to the beaches.

I remember talking with my father, a freight train conductor on the Pennsylvania Railroad, who told me that during the preparations for June 6 D-Day, railroad traffic to the port of Baltimore was almost unbelievable. He said the deadlines that had to be met were hard to imagine. He remembered taking trains which had originated in St. Louis and picking them up in Columbus, Ohio, and going nonstop all the way to the dock in Baltimore. He said the variety of equipment was enormous, and there were no excuses for being late, since the materials had to get to Baltimore on the dock and be loaded onto the transports, which were leaving at 8 AM the next morning, come hell or high water. The pressure on all the workers was tremendous, since the materials had to be on the transports in order for them to get into the convoys leaving to cross the Atlantic on time.

I reflect back on the planning groups at Pearl Harbor who coordinated all the needs for combat and support of equipment, food, ammunition, clothing, and medical supplies for the 750,000 men who were involved in the Marianas operation. The greater part of these planners from the various services probably averaged between 35 and 45 years of age. All of them had several years prior experience in the military, and Major Anderson, who was in charge of this operation, remarked to me at one time that many of these men had graduated from college in 1930, '31 or '32 and because of the Depression had been unable to find a job. Consequently, many of them had opted to make a career in the nation's military services. In many ways, these men performed near miracles in terms of planning, organizing, and identifying all the various needs for the Marianas operation several months in advance. It was vital to coordinate the orders for ships that hadn't been built, men who had not been recruited or drafted for service and trained, had to be accomplished with no exceptions or failures.

The only delay that I was aware of in all the operations that were conducted in the Pacific Ocean occurred on Iwo Jima. We had landed on Iwo on Monday, February 19, and on Thursday of that week orders were given to curtail partially the firing of our 105's. The reason given was that we were, running short of ammunition and that the ship carrying the 105 ammunition was just two days late. If I look at the distance from the West Coast of the United States to Iwo Jima, being two days late as far as we were concerned was an outstanding accomplishment. I should add that this little blip did not interfere with our combat efforts on the island. There was the same pressure within our country to get materials from manufacturing plants to the seaports which shipped millions of tons of equipment, material and food supplies to the rest of the world.

A little known aspect of the creation of the eight transcontinental railroads running from the Mississippi River to the Pacific Ocean was a clause in the law which subsidized the construction of these roads. The contracts dating from 1862 granted these railroads 10 square miles in alternate sections along the routes as well as direct allocation of funds with the amount determined by the terrain. In other words, laying railroad tracks through the mountains would be much more expensive and therefore valuable than putting the same track down in the plains. The clause to which I refer stated that inasmuch as the government and people of the United States were making it possible with these land and money grants to build the roads, that in the event the United States would ever need to use these roads for transporting military equipment in case of war, the railroads would transport these needs and troops at 50% of their regular rate. It has been estimated that in addition to the land grants the federal government had granted the transcontinental companies approximately $456 million. Given the length and duration of the war in the Pacific, it became very clear that the American public recovered many times over the original construction costs.

The invasion

The plan for the invasion of Saipan involved two Marine divisions, the Second and Fourth, and the Twenty-seventh Army division. We intended to utilize the center of the island, Mt. Tapacho, to divide the areas of responsibility for each division. The landing was to take place on the southwest coast of Saipan with the Fourth Division on the right of the landing area and the Second Division on the left. There was a little town called Charan Kanoa in the landing area which had been totally demolished except for one round brick smokestack. After the landing, the Second Division was to move inland to the approximate area of Mount Tapacho and then swing towards the north, going up the west side of the island between the mountain and the beach. The Fourth Division was to continue straight across the island to the eastern shore and cut off the peninsula on the southeast corner of the island. The 27th Army Division was to come into the center between the two Marine divisions and maintain communications with and stay in direct contact with these other units. One Army regiment was to maintain the blockade of the Japanese troops in the southeastern peninsula. If they could be isolated, it would certainly limit any strategy of the defenders.

Admiral Spruance, commander of the naval battle group that conducted the bombardment of the landing areas, started three days before we arrived. I remember well that when we were in our landing craft, we passed beneath the shadow of the battleship Iowa. While we were headed for the beach and probably 80 yards away from the Iowa, a full broadside was fired. I always thought that when the big naval guns were fired, one would hear a very loud boom and that would be all there was to it. I was certainly mistaken, because when the broadside was fired, there was a sonic boom and as it passed over our landing craft, there was a tremendous crack. It sounded like a huge paddle had been brought down on the surface of the water with tremendous force. I think my ears were affected for a couple of days as a consequence. The first two waves landed without too much difficulty because of the strafing by our carrier planes, and the heavy bombardment was keeping Japanese gunners away from their weapons.

Saipan averaged about five miles across and slightly more than 12 miles going north-south. Korean labor battalions had built fortifications and grottos in the side of Mount Tapacho for the housing of their big guns. These large guns were mounted on wheels which looked like a railway car size. When they wanted to fire one of their weapons, steel doors which covered the entrance would open and the gun would come out mounted on rails. It would fire one round, immediately go back into its cave, and the doors would automatically close again. This would make it seem almost impossible to neutralize these weapons until our troops could get right up to the mouth of the cave.

It was at this point that the Marine air wing entered the picture under the leadership of Major Gregory "Pappy" Boyington. It was critical for him to know exactly how long the doors protecting the guns were actually open, and in order to determine this, several of his pilots flew over the area and timed the duration of how long their big guns were exposed.

Their judgment was that the doors were open approximately 65 to 70 seconds for the firing of these big guns. Their plan of attack was simple and in keeping with the daredevil attitude of Pappy's boys, as they were sometimes called. They put a 500-pound bomb on the bottom of their planes and circled at approximately 2000 feet in the air above the guns. When the doors opened, the pilot would go into an immediate full power dive and launch the 500-pound bomb before pulling his plane up from the dive. This was extremely dangerous, but over a period of two days they succeeded either in knocking the guns out or damaging the doors so severely that they were inoperable. Parenthetically, I would add that the air support given in the Battle of Tinian was a major contribution to reducing our casualties throughout that battle.

The two Marine divisions met their objectives on the first and second days moving past Charan Kanoa and reaching the eastern shore after isolating the enemy on the peninsula. On the fifth day, Japanese troops broke through the army lines that had kept them isolated in the peninsula and attacked the rear lines of the Fourth Division Marines. The 14th Regiment artillery gunners turned their weapons around, drastically shortened their fuses. and fired point-blank at the enemy troops. Other units came to the aid of the artillery and swept the area to make sure that all the enemy troops were either killed or captured.

As I went through this area looking for prisoners who might be wounded, I ran across two American soldiers who had been wounded by the Japanese. They were sitting and leaning against a tree trunk and appeared to be in shock. I had been talking with them for a few minutes when one of them suddenly blurted out that he and his buddy were very sorry that they had let the Marines down but that they had done their very best. I assured them that we were all fighting the same battle and that they needn't have anything to apologize for. I asked them where their officers were and they told me that they hadn't seen their company commander since the first day of landing. To the best of my knowledge, there were no Army officers present when the breakthrough occurred and during the intense fighting that followed. The problem was that nearly all of the Army officers were not with their troops but instead at the general's command center.

To further complicate the situation, when the two Marine divisions advanced in their respective areas, the Army troops were told to stay even and maintain liaison between the Marines on their right and left. When they failed to advance in the succeeding days along with the Marines, it exposed the respective flanks of the Marine forces to enemy penetration.

This was an intolerable situation which required drastic action. The solution was to remove the Army general in charge of the 27th division for failure to have his troops advance. There was a great deal of media attention given to this action on the part of the Marine commander. It was based on a lot of hearsay, and probably neither side was entirely right. I firmly believe and know from my own personal contacts with Army personnel that the ones I saw in combat were as brave as any other American servicemen regardless of branch of service.

The two worst situations on islands that I was on during the war were Saipan and Pelileu. Saipan had a reputation of being the most diseased area in the world, hosting such diseased as dengue fever, and I saw nothing to disabuse myself of that idea. It was exceedingly hot in the summer of 1944, and the undergrowth in many areas was almost soggy. There were of course other areas which were at a higher elevation where the ground was not as soft. I had the feeling many times that I was in the jungle with bugs of all kinds and high humidity both day and night. Most Marines would put mosquito nets over their helmets when eating to keep out the bugs.

I did not find any fresh water on the island, and I watched Japanese soldiers drink water out of little streams which must have been horribly polluted. Around the 15th or 16th day on the island, everyone was issued a new pair of boots, which we called boondockers. I didn't know what size we were getting, but I didn't hear anyone complain, so that the idea that one-size-fits-all may have been correct. I actually think there must have been at least two or three sizes that were distributed. They were sorely needed, as the dampness and water and humidity combined to make our shoes simply disintegrate.

I'm not sure of the exact date, but certainly by the end of the first two weeks, a detachment of Seabees came ashore, moved to the central southern part of the island, and immediately set to work to fix the air strip that the Japanese used. The first thing they did was o build a large mess hall for themselves which was well screened to keep out the bugs and which had a floor about two feet above ground surface. They accomplished all of this within a remarkably short time, and did so based on their experience that if their men had decent food , fewer of them would become ill. I am confident that all servicemen had great respect for the Seabees. They were experienced middle-aged men, for the most part, and thoroughly skilled in their individual trades.

As a consequence, they worked very rapidly in spite of the combat very close to where they were and accomplished much more than anyone would have expected. They took the totally inadequate airstrip that the Japanese had used and turned it into a vital airbase. In less than two weeks, they had sufficiently prepared the air strip so that it was available for use by the planes doing the strafing and bombing on Tinian. This was a distinct bonus for the Marines.

Below the airport area next to the southern shore of Saipan, the various artillery units set up shop for the invasion of Tinian. Strung along the southern shore were the artillery regiments of the Second and Fourth Marine divisions and the 27th Army division. In addition, the Marine Fifth Corps artillery was also present. The presence of this land-based artillery and a working air strip close at hand contributed immensely to our success on Tinian, with far fewer casualties than we suffered on Saipan.

The usual practice on the front lines was to schedule jumping off time each morning between 7:30 and 9:00 AM. Before the lines moved, there was an artillery barrage laid down in the areas ahead of our front lines which may have lasted from 20 to 30 minutes, depending on the terrain. Each day had a target to achieve, and on our maps these were reflected as the 0-1 line for the first day, successively counted up for each day. These battle plans were carefully laid out for each battalion, which was usually maintained by a regimental commander who had the rank of colonel. Of course these plans could be modified to fit a particular situation that might develop. It was my understanding that the Saipan operation adhered closely to the original plans.

The jumping-off time was frequently altered so as to keep the enemy off balance as to when the attack might resume. On several occasions, the commanding officer of the battalion would be on the front lines with his troops when they jumped off for the day. I remember hearing a general remind the battalion commander that he was too valuable to be on the front lines himself, since it was his responsibility to maintain order and give the necessary commands as the battle evolved. I will remember as long as I live the response to this admonition frequently given by one colonel. He stated very simply that if he were going to order his men into battle, the least he could do was to be at the front lines when his troops started every day.

The Koreans

The shelling of the beaches prior to our landing hastened the onset of labor for several Korean expectant mothers. They came into our lines, assisted by their friends, pleading that something be done. Fortunately we had a Navy doctor named Stewart who kept his wits about him and handled the situation. Since there were no tents available, he utilized tarps thrown over what was left of some trees that had been destroyed by the combat. In short order he found some stretchers and supports to put them on, as if they were in an operating room in a hospital. He then delivered three or four infants within a matter of two or three hours.

The friends of these new mothers helped out with taking care of the new infants as Dr. Stewart moved from one stretcher to another. He needed medical information about these women and so my medical vocabulary was challenged. Fortunately, the other women were of great assistance in providing the information. As an interpreter I had to figure out how I could use simple words to find out how many months pregnant each of these prospective mothers was, whether this was their first child, and if they had any illnesses of which were aware.

Even today I find it almost impossible to adequately describe the situation. The women were fearful and had been indoctrinated with how cruel Americans are and how badly we would treat them. What they found was just the opposite, an American doctor performing near miracles under very difficult conditions. When I left the makeshift operating conditions I was not only thankful for the presence of Dr. Stewart but gratified by the sincere appreciation shown by these women. The efforts of our doctors and corpsmen to help not only our own troops but other human beings did more to raise the appreciation and status of the United States in foreign countries than almost anything else that we could imagine.

Later, when Dr. Stewart met a fellow physician, a chest surgeon from Manchuria who had trained at Mukden, I was able to translate for them for an hour or two. It was a humbling experience, trying to deal with medical terms rather than military ones.

Meanwhile, as the two Marine divisions moved northward on Saipan on each side of Mt. Tapacho, we encountered ever increasing numbers of civilians far beyond our pre-invasion estimates. As we planned the invasion, one of the concerns was the presence on Saipan of many thousands of Koreans who had been moved there as labor battalions used for the construction of defense installations around Mt. Tapacho. The town of

Garapan on the western shore in the northern sector had a population of 10,000 or more made up of the families of these Korean workers. Since these were forced labor groups under the Japanese military, the decision was made that they should be treated as noncombatants.

Consequently, this would require some personnel who could speak their language. Fortunately, there was a small Korean community on the island of Oahu which housed its own church. The priest of this church, Father Cho, was just past 60 years of age and a bachelor living alone in a modest home on Kauai Street close to his church. I visited him several times before the convoy left Pearl Harbor on the first of May.

Father Cho had received his doctorate in theology from the University of Wisconsin and fully understood not only the need to help fellow Koreans but the dangers entailed in entering a combat zone. He had a relaxed smile on his face at all times and was always quick to point out the humor of any situation. These qualities were sorely tried on Saipan.

Once the first few days of the battle had passed, Korean civilians began streaming through our lines desperately seeking shelter from the combat going on around them. They had no water and some had not eaten anything for four or five days. Most were terrified and in pitiful condition. We designated an area behind our lines to the west of Mt. Tapacho, where we directed them to go. It was at this point that Father Cho became the man of the hour. He walked among these refugees and continually assured them that everything would be okay.

I will never understand how he managed this chaotic situation, but within two hours large kettles had appeared from somewhere and large hot rice balls were soon being made and jeeps with water tanks appeared seemingly out of nowhere. I later discovered that Father Cho had the foresight to make arrangements for these basic needs.

We had assigned a young Marine private from Cleveland, Ohio, to be the bodyguard for Father Cho and instructed him that he was never to leave his side. There was some uneasiness that he might be taken for the enemy by other Marines. I saw Father Cho a few times during his stay on Saipan, and he was continually helping to assure these civilians that everything would be all right. They followed him around in the camp as their savior. I thought more than once that this must have been very similar to times when Christ walked on this earth. He suffered physically from the extreme heat and the jungle humidity but I never heard a single word of complaint during the entire period.

The young Marine bodyguard proved to be very resourceful. About the tenth day on the island, he appeared with a Jeep on which he had repainted Marine numbers and logos. He was able to drive "Fasa Cho-san" around on Saipan and save him from too much physical exertion in the intensive heat and humidity that was Saipan that summer. When it was time to return to rest base the Jeep was loaded onto the transport with the others and returned to rest base. Our PFC drove it around there for three weeks before a motor pool sergeant noticed there was an extra vehicle.

Father Cho stayed on Saipan after the battle had ended in the middle of July and assisted in acting as the interpreter for our doctors who had toiled for many long days under very difficult conditions. Father Cho contributed so much to not only his fellow Koreans but to everyone on the island.

Several months later I was able to visit him again at his home in Honolulu. He still had the same appearance although he admitted that he did not have the stamina once he finished his duties on Saipan. He had resumed his duties as a priest and spoke very modestly about his activities in the war. I learned that he had said nothing about his experiences to his parishioners so I was very glad that I could tell them about his great contributions for which the Marine Corps and U.S. government were very proud and grateful for his contributions.

The Koreans who worked for the Japanese as laborers building fortifications were delighted by the landing of our forces. Toward the end of the struggle, I saw a group of them and tried to get them to form lines so we could get them under Father Cho's care. I asked them to count off, and they began to, but in Japanese. Knowing just a little Korean, I stopped them and asked them to continue in Korean, as they would now be treated as Korean and not under the Japanese. I saw some smiles, and they counted off with gusto in their own tongue. I then announced that after the war, Korea would be independent, and they cheered and marched off in good order.

A very real complication occurred frequently when our front lines passed a cave entrance on the side of Mount Tapacho. Some of these entrances were large enough to drive a regular truck into. Others were smaller and would permit two people at a time to walk in or out. The large caves with the big entrances were frequently four or five levels deep, dug into the side of the mountain. The descent from the ground level of a cave to the next one below was made by having a two-foot wide ledge around the side wall of the area from which to descend. I remember going into the second and third levels of these caves and estimating that the area across each level would be about 24 by 24 feet square. The Japanese stored many of their supplies in these caves with certain levels being designated for medical supplies or food or even water. The ammunition would not be in these large cave areas but in more easily hidden locations near where they anticipated would be necessary in battle.

When we passed these cave entrances it was absolutely necessary that we determine if there were enemy troops inside on any of the levels of the caves, or whether there were civilians who were using the caves to protect themselves from the bombardments. In many instances when we went into the cave, we could hear people talking and children crying on one of the lower levels. We tried to talk to them either from the first or the second level and explain to them that we would not hurt them and that we would help any of their people who had been wounded or who were sick and that we had water and food to provide for them if they should decide to come up.

After a few minutes urging them to please come up because we would have to close the entrance. I would then ask them to send up one or two men to talk with us and let them decide that it would be safe for all of them to come up and get food and water. Usually after a few minutes one or two of the men would come hesitantly up from a lower-level. It would be impossible to describe the terror in the eyes of these individuals. They hugged the wall as if they were going to fall off and walked very carefully since they had no idea of what it would be like when they got to our level. The best definition of absolute stark terror that I ever saw was in the eyes of these individuals.

One of the first things we did was to ask them to sit down so we could talk, and we proceeded to give them water, which they gulped down hurriedly. In some instances, we were partially successful and perhaps 20 or 30 individuals would come up. We usually had a corpsman standing by outside the cave to treat anyone who may have been wounded.

Our front lines had already passed, by so the inhabitants would not have to worry about Japanese soldiers. I was astounded they asked about safety, but we assured them we would absolutely protect them from enemy action.

Sometimes we had to seal the cave entrance to prevent our troops being attacked from the rear. I was very sad when we had to do this, because I thought we might be burying these people alive. About a month later, though, I was informed that the numbers of civilians on Saipan were in excess of 20,000, and the caves must have had exits from the lower levels. Even for several months after we left the island, there were still Korean civilians appearing before our garrison troops needing help.

The Japanese government had given its own citizens assurances that they would be protected from any enemy action. But the Jimmy Doolittle raid in early 1942 that was done in retaliation for Pearl Harbor put caused some real dissatisfaction among the Japanese public, and this increased as news from the war fronts were becoming totally negative for them. The Joint Intelligence Center at Pearl Harbor was convinced that the Marianas campaign would have a great political effect in the Japanese homeland.

To prove that it could protect the people in the Japanese homeland, the Japanese planned an attack, first from the air and then from its battle fleet. As a consequence, while Admiral Spruance and his bombardment fleet were engaged with the defense emplacements on Saipan in the first few days of the operation, word came that the Japanese battle fleet had put to sea headed for Saipan and Guam. When we heard that the Japanese battle fleet was headed towards the Marianas, Admiral Spruance was ordered to take his bombardment fleet and retreat to the east to avoid contact with the Japanese battle fleet. The next day, there were none of our ships visible off the coast of Saipan.

We had a temporary barbed wire area to handle Japanese prisoners for a short time before sending them out to one of our ships. That evening when I was down where the prisoners were, I noticed one

Japanese soldier squatting and looking out to sea. It dawned on me that the Japanese communications system was still working and getting messages to Saipan. This particular soldier had heard the news of the battle and was looking out to sea waiting for the Japanese fleet to show up. This irritated me, and so I stood there by this Japanese soldier for a few minutes and then muttered "Not yet, huh?" and walked off.

Turkey Shoot

About 400 miles from where we were on Saipan, the great Marianas Turkey Shoot was about to take place. The Japanese carrier fleet had emerged and was aiming at Guam, with the intention of making a strike on the American fleet and then landing at Guam to be refueled and re-armed with ammunition to return and strike at the American fleet a second time. This was a good strategy, but to Admiral Marc Mitscher, it provided an opportunity to get at the Japanese naval aircraft. He first pulled his fleet of carriers back to the north out of the intended path of the Japanese pilots; and then sent his dive bombers to Guam, where they would proceed to drop bombs all over the air strips. This was intended to prevent any landing by the Japanese pilots for refueling, which meant they would not have enough fuel to get back to their carriers.

On June 19, Mitscher's strategy worked. After the Japanese pilots had engaged our fighter planes, they proceeded to Guam to land for refueling. Unfortunately, the airstrip on which they were going to land had been almost totally destroyed, with large bomb craters on the runways, and there was no other choice at that stage except to crash. American pilots had a field day and destroyed over 400 Japanese aircraft in the afternoon and evening.

The Japanese carrier fleet had learned of the disaster and had reversed course to head out of danger. Admiral Mitscher was aware of this and ordered his bombers to take off and try to overtake the fleeing Japanese carriers. It was now late in the afternoon, and he realized that it would be a very close call for his pilots to get back for a safe landing on his carriers while it was still daylight. He determined that it was worth the risk, and after his bombers had taken off, he ordered the entire fleet of our carriers plus their escorts to head west after the Japanese fleet as fast as possible. He knew that his fleet could never cover the distance to the enemy fleet; but if he could move them 50 or 60 miles closer, it would shorten the distance that his own pilots would have to fly in order to get back to the carriers for a safe landing.

The American carrier planes did overtake the fleeing Japanese fleet and inflict serious damage. They had flown almost maximum range for their aircraft when they headed back towards their fleet. As it was growing dark, the possibility of these planes not being able to land caused Admiral Mitscher to order all his carriers and protective screens of destroyers and destroyer escorts in the entire area to turn on all our lights. The Admiral was willing to take this risk in enemy waters to save his pilots, for which I'm sure they have been eternally grateful.

Most of our planes made it back and landed safely on the well-lit carrier decks. Those who had to ditch because they were out of fuel were in most instances picked up safely. The significance of this Turkey Shoot was not just that it was an American victory but also the death knell of any Japanese carrier attacks for the rest of war. This made a profound difference for the whole Pacific Theater, but particularly in the Iwo Jima operation. Admiral William "Bull" Halsey's battle fleet meanwhile had taken off in pursuit of the retreating Japanese battle fleet and succeeded in inflicting some damage before darkness ended the engagement.

Naval Marshall Yamamoto's fears had been fulfilled, and the tremendous productive capacity of the United States proved decisive in almost every phase of naval warfare from January 1944 to the end of the war.

One of the saddest events in the Pacific War occurred near the end of the struggle on Saipan. I had earlier mentioned that there were large numbers of Korean and some Japanese civilians on the island. Some of them had moved, probably at night, to the northern sector for safety. As the front lines of our troops moved ever northward, they continued to retreat until they had reached the northern coast. In that area, the land dropped abruptly nearly 1500 feet almost straight down to a very rugged rocky shore.

To our dismay, several hundred civilians had congregated near these cliffs, called Marpi Point, with their children. They were totally convinced that the Americans would torture them and resort to all kinds of barbarities. Only recently, in 2008, has it been learned that the

Emperor had sent a message to all the civilians that if they took their own lives in an honorable fashion, they would be treated with the same honor as Japanese soldiers who had died for their Emperor.

Many of these civilians picked up their children with their wives and jumped off the cliff down on the rocky coast below. In an attempt to prevent this from continuing, we had the fire chief of Garapan, who was well known to everyone, stand on the prow of a small boat and get as close as possible to the rocky shore. He had a large megaphone and stood in clear view so that all could recognize him. He pleaded with the people not to jump. He promised them the Americans would not mistreat them in any way and that they had been lied to by the Japanese army officials.

Unfortunately they were so terrified that they continued to leap off the cliff. I saw some of our Marines who were 400-500 yards south of the shoreline break into a run to try to stop this needless loss of life, but to no avail. It was estimated that nearly 1500 to 2000 lost their lives by jumping to their death.

The stark contrast between fighting the enemy and then trying to save lives was especially bitter for all to accept. I believe that all of our troops throughout the world suffered over the loss of humanity. The best ambassadors for our nation during World War II were our troops, who shared their rations and food with innocent civilians who were caught up in the turmoil of fighting, regardless of the combat area in which they were engaged.

The fall of Saipan and the almost total destruction of all Japanese carriers and the loss of their pilots constituted a severe blow to the Empire of Japan. The close relationship between the military leaders and the civilian government in Japan since the Meiji Constitution of 1889 had seen the two become fully integrated during the second year of the war, as General Tojo Hideki, Commander in Chief of the nation's armed forces, became prime minister of the national government. Faced with the reality of the loss of Saipan and the near total destruction of Japan's naval power, Gen. Tojo submitted his resignation to the Emperor, and it was accepted. The continuing debacle in the Marianas with the loss of Tinian and Guam simply added to the disgrace in which he was held. As a consequence of these losses, the Japanese military leadership saw the upcoming invasion of the homeland, and they undertook vigorous efforts to build up the defenses of

Iwo Jima and Okinawa, thinking that the Americans would approach Japan from one or the other of these directions and needed a base for further operations when they invaded the main islands of Japan.

Tinian

Of all the invasions in the Pacific Theater, there was none that went as smoothly as the attack on Tinian. This was due to several factors, and probably the most important was that, once Saipan had been taken, it permitted our forces to line up land-based artillery along the southern shore of Saipan to fire directly across at the northern part of Tinian, which was only a distance of two and three-quarter miles. The combined artillery units came from the Second and Fourth Marine divisions, the Twenty-seventh Army division and the V Amphibious Corps. In all, there were 14 different artillery units on the southern shore of Saipan.

Of almost equal importance, the invasion plan of assault for Tinian provided for a mock invasion to be carried out on the southwest coast of the island, with the aim of keeping enemy forces in the southern part of the island while the real landing took place through a narrow gap in the coral reef along the northwestern shoreline.

When we were headed towards the beach to land, one Marine said it "sounded like Gene Krupa playing the drums." That seemed like an apt description, as the land-based artillery on Saipan maintained a terrific bombardment of the northern two miles of Trinian. This served not only to keep the beachhead protected but also prevented the Japanese from making troop movements towards the northern part where we were landing. By nightfall, we had landed sufficient forces to establish the beachhead and to construct a 0-1 line about 800 yards inland.

The battle plan of Colonel Evans Fordyce Carlson envisioned that the enemy would try to counterattack during the night to wipe out the assault forces on the beaches. To prepare for this, our troops put up two lines of barbed wire in front of our lines. The first line was approximately 50 yards in front of our troops and consisted of some loosely strung wire with a few tin cans attached. The second line was about 30 yards in front, firmly constructed with four levels of wire embedded with posts and sandbags. We had placed machine guns on the flanks of our lines so that our lines of fire would intersect at a distance of 20 yards.

It was Carlson's idea that the enemy would wait until 1:00 or 2:00 AM and then launch an all-out charge at our lines. He thought the enemy would encounter the very weak first barbed wire with the tin cans as being the only one, and that once they had reformed their lines, they would make a full direct assault. We could hear a few tin cans being rattled shortly after 1:00 AM, and shortly thereafter the enemy made an all-out charge and was nearly impaled on the second barbed wire line. I did not know what the total enemy losses were that night, but we lost two men and counted over 450 enemy dead in front of our lines. The estimate was that enemy wounded exceeded the number killed by at least 600 or more.

This action on the first night of the Tinian invasion broke the backbone of the enemy resistance. The disastrous all-out attempt to repel our invasion on the beachhead did not produce results. When we landed on Iwo Jima six months later, General Kurabayashi's defense was entirely different.

In addition to having the support of land-based artillery on Saipan, the arrival of P-47s to furnish air support was a major factor in keeping our casualties to a minimum. These aircraft could fly slowly enough to be highly effective in strafing enemy lines immediately before we attacked each morning. The P-47s carried eight machine guns attached under the wing tips, as well as cannon in the nose and a 500-pound bomb under the fuselage. The strafing of the enemy front lines was devastating, not only in that it neutralized any active resistance but also by demoralizing their front line troops. The subsequent advance by our troops was made much easier because many of the enemy troops were still suffering the effects of the assault from the air.

While the victory on Tinian was assured by the third day, several officers of the Fourteenth Artillery Battalion were killed when an enemy shell exploded in their fox hole.

The *USS California* experienced misfortune on two occasions in the Marianas operation. During pre-invasion maneuvers in the Central Pacific, the battleship ran aground, suffering serious damage to its prow. When the repairs were finished, the ship arrived in time to support the landing on Tinian. Its targets were along the hilly area on the southwest part of the island. Apparently, the decision was made to move in closer to shore and use smaller guns than the 16-inch batteries. A Japanese shell landed directly on one of the gun turrets, resulting in the death of 50 or more of our crew. Needless to say, the California pulled back some distance and used its big guns to completely decimate the Japanese battery.

One of the saddest things I witnessed near the end of the Tinian struggle occurred on the next-to-last day. About ten o'clock that morning, our troops were moving south against minimal resistance. We noticed that about 300 yards in front of our lines there were a lot of civilians running around in almost total disarray. Incredibly, a dozen or so Japanese soldiers were assembling a large number of these men, women, and children into the center of the field and running around them with ropes, tying them all together. They then carried two or three ammo boxes into the middle and proceeded to blow everyone up. When some of our troops saw what was happening, they started to run to prevent it. It was to no avail. I talked with three of the few survivors, who believed that we would torture them if they were captured. Our corpsmen tried to do what they could, but I know that two of the survivors died within a few minutes. It was a repeat of the Marpi Point suicides on Saipan.

The landing on Tinian was made on July 24, since our invasion was delayed until the forces had started the assault on Guam on July 21 and felt they could handle that battle without needing any reinforcements. The Turkey Shoot had ended a month before, and the enemy fleets had long since retreated, either west of the Philippines or to ports on Okinawa or southern Japan.

The existence of nearly all the Chamoros in the Marianas on Guam was a real asset for our forces, since they volunteered to do anything the Marines wanted or needed. I only heard words of praise from fellow Marines for the conduct of the Chamoros that summer.

I was traveling to Japan at the turn of the twenty-first century and stopped overnight in Guam. I was amazed at the great difference in the condition of the island since the war, and the many modifications of the terrain and new buildings. The beaches where the assault forces landed have been altered almost beyond recognition. When I was preparing to leave for the airport the next morning, I asked my taxi driver about some of the changes.

He got very excited and told me that that day was the major holiday celebration of the year, since it was the date of our landing in 1944.

During our conversation, he told me that Japanese businessmen had bought quite a bit of land and built hotels for Japanese honeymooners to spend their time on Guam. Somewhat bitterly, he noted that when the Japanese hotel executives came to buy the land, they promised that this would be a great boon to the local economy. But the hotels hired all their personnel from Japan, only Japanese is spoken in the hotels or on the grounds surrounding them, and even the menus are printed in Japanese. As a consequence, the rebuilding has created extremely little benefit for the native Chamoros.

I had commitments which I could not break, to the disappointment of my taxi driver, since he said I could have ridden in the parade and had hundreds of people thank me for freeing them from the Japanese. I almost had to hand-wrestle him to pay the fare to the airport. I have never had a welcome as warm as my short stay in Guam.

11

IWO JIMA

During the summer of 1944, when the battle of the Marianas was in progress, we came across some documents indicating that the estimated defense forces on Iwo Jima totaled approximately 2500 troops. In December of that year, the Japanese had moved some first-rate troops in from the Manchurian area, and total troop strength was estimated at more than 20,000. In addition, troop deployments on Okinawa were rapidly expanding. It was apparent that the Japanese knew that the battle for their very homeland was in the near future. Additional defensive structures were being assembled. and Lt. General Kuribayashi Tadamichi was given the command of the island, with orders to defend it to the last man if necessary. In slightly more than seven months, he had conceived a different plan of defense and cleverly situated his troop deployment and defensive positions for maximum advantage.

Over the summer months, Gen. Kuribayashi's chief aide was Major Yoshitake Horie, who had functioned at army headquarters in Tokyo. He had been wounded earlier in China and had graduated from the War College in 1942. In 1965 he published a diary of his activities from that time until the end of the war. Upon his appointment as aide to General Kuribayashi, he worked diligently to gather everything the latter needed to prepare Iwo Jima's defense.

After the bombing from Tinian was increased after December 1, 1944, it became impossible to send any supplies to Iwo Jima during the day. Therefore, Yoshitake devised a plan to take the large cargo ships from Hiroshima and unload them at Chichi, Jima approximately 200 miles north of Iwo Jima. At that point, the large ship would be unloaded on the dock.

Later that evening, the supplies were reloaded onto much smaller but faster ships for transfer to Iwo at night.

Once they had arrived, the ships were unloaded as quickly as possible so they could make a return run back to Chichi Jima before the American bombers made their daily raids.

The civilian population of Iwo Jima had long since been evacuated back to the mainland, and the labor force used to perform all the unloading and reloading was made up of retired servicemen. Many complained about the long hours and hard labor, but Yoshitake persisted in getting the job done. By the middle of February, the defending Japanese forces numbered 22,000, and rations and water sufficient for 40 days had been accumulated before the upcoming battle. Yoshitake had made many trips back to beg the high command in Tokyo for more supplies and was quite successful. General Kuribayashi was quite pleased with his efforts.

On February 16, Yoshitake returned to Chichi Jima to handle a few issues. Fortunately for him, the American carrier planes were engaged in the final bombing and strafing operations prior to the landing on February 19. He therefore was unable to get back to Iwo Jima, and so he lived until 1967. Some of his notes and letters have appeared in the *Marine Gazette* in the past.

The forces that were to attack this bastion began to gather late in December of 1944, and the actual battle for Iwo began that month. The opening phase consisted of combined naval and air action. On two occasions in December, naval battle echelons subjected the island to bombardment while attempting to locate enemy artillery positions. The air attacks, usually consisting of B-24s and on a few occasions B-29s, came from both Saipan and Tinian. Captured enemy documents during the invasion showed that softening-up phase activity had been continuous for 70 days prior to the landing on February 19. They also showed that only two enemy casualties had been suffered during the entire period. One soldier had been killed by strafing when he chose to run across the airfield during an air raid and the other by shrapnel.

During January and February, the intensity and frequency of both naval and air bombardments increased. Meanwhile, the total invasion forces were assembling at Saipan. Between February 12 and 16, carrier planes brought additional tonnage of bombs and strafing to bear on the defenders.

Navy Seals made several probes along the beaches night to determine the extent of underwater obstacles which could be encountered by the assault waves. Naval support units (battleships, cruisers and some destroyers) had already been assigned specific areas on the island grid and had moved into place when the assault waves left the Saipan area according to schedule on February 16.

The general plan reflected our belief that Iwo Jima and Okinawa would be the last islands to be taken before the actual invasion of the Japanese homeland would begin. Iwo Jima was to be an all-Marine operation, with the Fourth and Fifth Divisions making the assault and the Third Division held at sea in reserve. The landing was to occur on the southeast beaches of the island, with the Fifth Division on the left and the Fourth on the right. The Fifth was to push as rapidly as possible straight across the neck of the island to the western shore and isolate Mt. Surabachi from any and all contact with other enemy forces. The Fourth was to move straight in to gain control of Motoyama Airstrip No. and then turn right toward the second airstrip. It is interesting to note that the original plans anticipated that the Fourth Division would be replaced by the Third Division on the fifth day to finish the battle. The Fourth was then scheduled to return to Saipan to get whatever equipment was necessary for the initial assault on Okinawa on March 1.

The critical importance of fielding a successful invasion this close to the homeland dictated that every effort be made to prevent enemy aircraft from attacking our forces on the ground.

This mission was given to Admiral Marc Mitscher's Carrier Task Force 58. When we landed on Iwo Jima in February, 1945 the American carrier fleet under Adm. Mitscher was charged with the responsibility for neutralizing every Japanese air base and facility from Tokyo all the way south around Kyushu. This was achieved in a remarkably short time, which permitted more carrier air support for the troops on Iwo. This meant that his carrier fleet would be stretched from Tokyo in a great arc southward to the southern end of Kyushu. I still gasp at the enormity of this endeavor, because it would place our carriers within 20 to 30 miles offshore from all major military and naval air installations in the Japanese homeland. In addition, the carrier fleet was to furnish approximately 50 planes in support of the ground troops on Iwo Jima twice a day for targeted missions.

The voyage from Saipan to Iwo was unusually rough, with seas running high, and there was some concern about D-day weather. I remember seeing the battleship Missouri, weighing 60,000 tons, thrown up by the force of the waves and coming down with a great thud each time, making everyone aware of the power of the ocean. The morning of the 19th dawned clear, with only moderate wave action, and the landings went off pretty close to schedule. The usual air strikes and naval bombardment had clearly kept the enemy pinned down in caves or bunkers, preventing any substantial fire on the assault waves getting ashore.

The immediate difficulty was discovering that Iwo's beaches consisted of mostly volcanic ash intermixed with black sand. The heavily laden troops sunk into the ground with every step, and it took a real effort to just make it up the slope of the beach. If they scooped out a hole to give them temporary cover, it at once began to fill in and cave in on the sides. I am not sure, but I think the average Marine going ashore was probably carrying 40 to 50 pounds of weapons, ammunition, and backpack when he got out of the landing craft. The physical exertion required just to keep going on the volcanic sandy beaches was extraordinary. All mechanical equipment bogged down within 20 or 30 yards of the beach. Eventually, perforated aluminum air strips were brought ashore and laid on top of the ground to enable vehicles to get enough traction to move ever so slowly up the slopes.

To add to the difficulties encountered early in the fighting, we found that Motoyama No. 1 airstrip, whose name translates as Little Mountain, was located approximately 20 feet above us. This meant that ladders had to be brought in to enable our troops to just get up to the edge of the air strip. But the Japanese had machine gun emplacements set up within 25 yards of the rim, so that as Marines came up off the ladders, they were faced with direct enemy fire.

We eventually found a way to the ends of the airstrip. This enabled us to attack the pillboxes by triangulating on them from two diagonals. But this also meant that we had to depend on air support to strafe the pillboxes that were firing on us, so we could advance without a total slaughter.

It was a textbook case of coordination. Yellow disks on the back of the Marines on the front line helped spotters locate the line of combat on the map, then get that message to the ship, which would pass in along to the airplanes to strafe. It was logistics, and showed the skills of the Signal Corps. And it demonstrates how well-trained the Marine Corps was and is. It is a thing of beauty—they are totally coordinated in working toward a goal. They know what they are doing, and help each other. They are a unit.

We paid a high price in Marine casualties to accomplish just getting onto the airstrip. Though the casualties were high, gradually the gun emplacements were knocked out and our advance onto the air strip proceeded.

The Fifth Division on the left moved straight ahead, seeking to get to the western shore of the island as rapidly as possible. Japanese gun emplacements in caves, holes and crevices among the rocks poured fire down on the Marines as they gradually edged their way across the rough terrain. Great difficulties continued to plague the troops in seeking to maintain contact on their flanks. The topography was so rugged and uneven that, on occasion, Marines in one area were looking down on others in their vicinity. Once they reached the west coast across the neck of the island, isolating Surabachi, they began the tremendous effort to gain control of the mountain. The Japanese had great observation points for their artillery not only on Surabachi but also at other locations in the northern part of Iwo Jima.

By the end of the first day, the Fifth Division had achieved its first objective in reaching the western side of the island. The Fourth had gained control of Motoyama No 1 airstrip.

The intensity of enemy fire had steadily increased from mid-morning and continued into the evening. Now, as the Marines were establishing their defense parameters for the night, the Japanese lowered their antiaircraft guns to fire over the their heads. This provided a steady shower of shrapnel on all areas along the beaches until well after midnight. The hissing sound made by shrapnel as it hit the volcanic ash made one feel as if we were targets in a shooting gallery.

Another interpreter, Tom Smith, and I shared a foxhole that night with our packs on our backs and helmets on. We each faced outwards to guard against any night time enemy attack. About 1:30 AM, I felt some shrapnel just scraping the back of my helmet. I was thinking that the shrapnel must have hit Tom in the head and killed him. There was no noise or movement for a couple of minutes, and then I heard groping around and Tom softly calling my name. He thought the same thing had happened to me. We got the chunk of shrapnel out of the volcanic ash in the morning and discovered it was an irregular four-or-five-inch hunk of metal. It had come down exactly between our helmets.

The experience of the first day proved to be an omen as to how the battle was to go for many days. And Iwo was costly real estate not only on the first day but throughout the entire battle. The struggles of the Fifth Division in wrenching Mt. Surabachi from enemy hands represented some of the fiercest fighting in the entire Pacific Theater. Our total arsenal of weapons was thrown into the effort to dislodge the enemy from this fortress. Naval aircraft made frequent bombing runs, often at great risk. Destroyers came perilously close to the sheer face of the mountain to fire point blank at enemy gun emplacements. Ground troops struggled in almost hand-to-hand combat as they inched their way up the rocky slopes.

Mitscher's Carrier Task Force not only furnished 50 planes at 8:00 AM and 1:00 PM to make bombing and strafing runs called up by the ground troops, but by the fourth day his fleet was offering to send 100 planes every hour on the hour for additional support to the Marines on the ground.

The flag flies

Fortunately, there were no defensive installations in the top 40 or 50 feet of Surabachi. The success in gaining the summit has been immortalized by the photographs and commemorative statuary well known to all. To the troops on the ground, the sight of the flag on top of Surabachi was not only a great morale booster, it signified the end of the situation in which enemy spotters could direct their artillery and mortar fire at our forces moving to the north.

Joe Rosenthal's famous picture was taken while Joe was trying to climb upon a box to get a better view. When his aide, who was basically pushing him up the hill, yelled, "There she goes," Joe half-turned and snapped the photo with a camera hanging by his side. Joe said later that the exposure was 1/400th of a second, and it was an instance that changed history, the iconic picture of World War II.

The Marine Corps pictures show very clearly that the first flag had just been lowered and the famous one had risen almost simultaneously. When Secretary of the Navy James Forrestal saw the picture, he remarked, "This means there will be a Marine Corps for the next thousand years."

Descriptions of Iwo's topography show Surabachi as the center point of any attack on the island and that the remainder of its eight square miles gradually slope to the northern end of the island. That is the area we now faced. To the dismay of all concerned, the ground from the northern edge of Motoyama No. 1 consisted of innumerable rock formations aligned in a maze-like pattern, with 20-to-30 foot high sides running 100 or so feet long. Kuribayashi's defensive strategy utilized every bit of the confusing terrain. He had built pill boxes into the very rocky crags to house his largest guns, covering as many approaches as possible. We found tanks almost totally buried under large boulders, and rocks with turret guns fixed on openings in the craggy hills. Open areas were covered with cleverly placed triangular machine gun nests nestled among the large boulders.

Underneath the rocks, boulders and interminable little open areas, the Japanese had created a maze of caves with interlocking connections. The openings to these were generally just large enough to permit passage of individuals and boxes or bags packed with medical supplies and some arms and ammunition. The Japanese had even tried to construct some underground connecting tunnels within 1000 yards of the beach, but the shifting sands and volcanic matter made these untenable.

While the beach landings and the struggle going up Mt. Surabachi were difficult, it was the well planned intricate defense system above the first airstrip that not only lengthened the battle for control of the island but contributed to the ever-growing casualty lists.

For instance, at the immediate northern tip of Motoyama No. 1 was Hill 382, which became known as the "meatgrinder." For nearly 10 consecutive days, battalions of the Fourth Division attacked this strategic target, with disheartening results. Each time, the Marines got to the summit by noon, but thereafter enemy mortar fire drove them off after taking more casualties. Our flame-throwing tanks were thrown into these areas, and six-by-six trucks, each with 36 rocket mounts, were utilized. Each of these rocket launchers contained a square of tubes, six by six, mounted on its floor at a 45-degree angle. They would be loaded a few 100 yards behind the front lines and then make a dash to a firing spot behind a craggy hill area. One Marine with a compass would jump out and stand in front of the truck in order to align it at the desired direction. All the 36 rockets would then be fired simultaneously, and the rocket truck would back out and make a hasty retreat to the rear for reloading. Usually, within 20 to 30 seconds of the rocket firing, Japanese mortar shells would be launched into the area just deserted by the trucks. While the rockets would not knock out specific obstacles, they packed a powerful shock punch affecting anyone within a wide circle.

General Kuribayashi's strategy was well adapted to the terrain, and his troops never intentionally exposed their well-camouflaged positions. The intent was to make the Marines pay a heavy price in personnel to achieve even limited progress. That it was a well conceived idea was evidenced by the losses inflicted on us as the battle dragged on.

On the sixteenth day, some units had to be completely reorganized. The Second Battalion of the 24th Marines merged Easy and Fox companies into X Company, with a total of 65 men. George Company itself had only 65 still standing. This meant that only a total of 130 men in those companies had not been killed or wounded in the first 15 days. Many specialist troops were transferred into these depleted units to maintain at least 60% combat level efficiency. Replacements arrived and filled in the gaps to the best of their ability. They seemed quite young and had only just finished several weeks of boot camp. They were assigned, almost on an individual basis, to veterans who tried to initiate them into the rigors of combat and teach them how to survive.

I remember one replacement that came to me after the short briefing session. He hesitantly asked me about using hand grenades, since he had been told that one should pull a pin before throwing it. When I asked if he had any grenades, he produced two unopened cartons from his satchel. I explained the process of handling grenades and sent him on his way. He had not known enough to take the grenade out of the carton before looking for the pin.

That these young men, with so little training, could be sent into battle was at best a saddening experience for many of the old timers. The sudden exposure to the intensity of the fighting on Iwo was a terrible shock for these young Marines. Many made the adjustment to combat, others had difficulty, and few suffered severe psychological trauma when they witnessed death for the first time.

I ran across two of these young men dragging their rifles on the ground and seemingly totally lost. They said that their lieutenant had just been killed right in front of them, and they were sobbing as they told me about it. I took them back behind our lines, got them calmed down, and later another Marine escorted them back to a temporary medical station.

It was difficult to witness the nearly total disintegration of other soldiers. Their speech became blurred, their eyes glazed over and their ability to walk without help had been lost. Little could be done with these men except to help them back to the beach for transport to the hospital ship lying offshore.

The prisoner

It was common practice that battlefield interrogations of the enemy were confined to identifying their military unit and getting other details which were of immediate importance for combat intelligence. They had never heard of the Geneva Convention rules and talked quite freely as they had no idea they would ever be captured. Additionally, they had been told over and over again that the Marines would torture them before killing them, and the terror in their eyes clearly reflected this. Therefore, we found that treating them with kindness and concern for their well-being only served to keep them in emotional shock. My first statement was that "for you, the war is over," and said that after we fixed their wounds and gave them some food, we would be sending them out to a ship in the harbor to be taken back to a nice island where they could sit out the rest of the war. While I was telling them this I would offer them a candy or fruit bar, water and a cigarette. But the most important words are those quoted above. We hoped that we could get the prisoner to think of his current situation as an entirely new one in his life, so he would know that he was free to think on his own.

It was near Hill 382 north of the Motoyama No. 1 airstrip that I had an experience with a prisoner that left me amazed and compelled me to write this book. The flag had been flying on top of Mt. Surabachi for more than a week, and shortly after our front line began to advance, we came across a Japanese soldier who was in a state of shell shock and was taken prisoner. I assured him that we would not kill or torture him in any way and he could join others of his comrades at the camp where he would be taken by one of our ships offshore.

After some further conversation about where he lived in Japan and how far he had gone in school, I asked him about his outfit and whether it was the 309th infantry battalion. He nodded his head in the affirmative and told me he was a member of a machine gun crew, and that his company had eight machine gun nests. He added that they were very short of water and food and that they had suffered a lot of casualties.

I then showed him a Japanese map of the island and asked him if he could find the area where he had been located. Since the terrain was so irregular, it was urgent that we locate enemy machine gun nests, mortar and artillery sites or firing locations so we could achieve greater accuracy in firing at positions not visible from our front lines. This was difficult as the scale on enemy maps was always different than ours and it required real skill to translate their locations to one of our maps.

We finally worked out where he had been the previous evening. He then pointed out the area where he last remembered his gun crew had been located. We found this spot on the map, and he continued by pointing out where the other machine gun nests were entrenched as best he could remember. At this juncture, our mortar officer looked over my shoulder at the Japanese map, converted the locations to his map, and called the target points back to his mortars. Within minutes, our mortars were dropping shells on the first two locations that the prisoner had pointed out. He looked up when heard the noise and then continued to point out the others. We sent the prisoner back to the beach from which he was taken out to the transport and ultimately to a prisoner of war camp.

After our front lines had passed the aforementioned areas, we checked out the locations that the prisoner had described and found that he had given us correct information on no fewer than five. I was quite amazed at the prisoner's attitude, especially after he knew we were firing at the very positions he had told us about. I knew that if a Marine had done the same thing, he probably would have been either shot on the spot or been convicted of treason. I also knew that American troops were clearly instructed that if they were captured, they could give their name, rank, serial number and nothing more.

The Japanese armed forces were constantly reminded that they were fighting for the emperor and that they should die fighting rather than surrender or be captured. To be taken prisoner was considered a total disgrace to one's family and an insult to the emperor. Given this indoctrination, it would be impossible to then turn around and explain how they should act if they were captured. I had previously heard other stories from prisoners about their battle experienced but never anything that would endanger their fellow troops.

We had learned that the Japanese troops were on half rations of food and water from the very first day we had landed. Over the next several days, the prisoners we took knew they were losing the battle and that there would be no relief for them from their homeland. General Kuribayashi had told his remaining troops that there was no help from Tokyo and that each one of them should try to kill at least 10 Americans before he died. He added that he had advised the Emperor of the situation and received the Emperor's thanks for his troops' defense of the island.

On the last day of the fighting on the northern coast of Iwo, we were making a sweep over areas we had taken in the previous two days, and one of our sergeants was making sure that every possible hiding place was investigated. When he peered into an opening about two feet in diameter, he was shot by an enemy soldier who must have been in hiding for at least two days. Within 30 seconds, we heard a grenade go off in the hole, which indicated that the soldier had committed suicide. Another Marine threw in one of our grenades just to make sure. The sergeant had received a wound to his shoulder, was taken to the hospital ship, and survived in good shape. He later went to Officer's Training School at Quantico and stayed in service for several years.

During the last 10 days on Iwo, the lines became much more irregular as we adjusted to the continuing terrain variations. On some occasions, we would carve out an area while moving to the north, and then stop that push, wheel to the right, and clear any enemy troops between our forces and the ocean. There were still more cave openings in the last two or three miles from our front lines to the beaches. We tried to investigate each one to make sure there were no more enemy soldiers hiding out or just waiting to shoot at us.

On some occasions I went into caves with a war dog and two or three Marines. We found very little of anything that would have been of use for any purpose. These caves matched the size of those on Saipan, and since there were no civilians on Iwo the only remaining items were a few uniforms and weapons, most of which were damaged and beyond use. Following two or three sweeps of these northernmost parts of the island, nearly everyone boarded ship for return to a rest base.

Ending the war

Part of the Japanese indoctrination of their troops and of their general population was that the superior spirit of the Japanese civilization would lead the nation to ever greater victories on the battlefield. It was even suggested that Japanese troops fought with such valor that even if the enemy might have some technical advantage it would make no difference in the long run. After the two atomic bombs had been dropped at Hiroshima and Nagasaki, Emperor Hirohito called for a top Council meeting in the bunker near the Imperial Palace. Of the six people who were in attendance at the Emperor's request were three military leaders and three senior domestic officers. After some extended debate the Emperor called for a vote as to whether or not the Japanese should surrender or keep on fighting. The vote on this issue was a tie with the three military leaders all voting to continue the war basing their opinion on the great spiritual strength of the Japanese nation. I could not believe that anyone could vote to continue the war after the two atomic bombs had been dropped and realizing that every major city in the nation had been almost burned beyond recognition. At this point, the Emperor took matters into his own hands and announced that this was his nation and that he could no longer ask his people to suffer so horribly. He therefore decided Japan would sue for peace and that he would make an announcement over radio to the entire nation of this decision. After he had made a taped statement there were still some military leaders who were trying to find the tape and destroy it. They knew that if the Japanese people heard their Emperor say that Japan was going to sue for peace that nobody would object and that the war would end.

Almost everyone was just simply worn out. I did not see or hear any Marine say much of anything to anyone else. It was as if we were all lost in our thoughts about friends who had been killed and perhaps wondering whether this struggle was really worth the cost. Nothing seemed to matter.

The next day at sea, we heard that the ship would stop at Saipan and drop off mail, so everyone was encouraged to write a letter or at least a postcard letting our families know that we were all right and going to a rest base. Very few must have responded to this announcement, so the next morning there was another plea to write to our families, since the mail would be flown back to the States and get there within two or three days. If we did not take advantage of this, it would be at least three weeks before there would be another chance.I wrote a card to my sister saying I was off that stinking island and was okay.

It was a very quiet group on the transport coming back. I was 21 years old, as were many others, and I think we all felt very old. We learned only later that more Marines were killed the first day on Iwo Jima than were killed on D Day in Europe. In fact, our total casualties on the Iwo Jima campaign were greater than the losses of the Japanese forces. The enemy losses were numbered at 22,000. I heard it told on the 65th anniversary of the battle at Quantico that the Iwo Jima battle was the only one in the entire war where our total casualties exceeded those of the enemy.

For Japan, it was different. Part of the Japanese indoctrination of their troops and of their general population was that the superior spirit of the Japanese civilization would lead the nation to ever greater victories on the battlefield. It was even suggested that Japanese troops fought with such valor that, even if the enemy might have some technical advantage, it would make no difference in the long run. After the two atomic bombs had been dropped at Hiroshima and Nagasaki, Emperor Hirohito called for a top council meeting in the bunker near the Imperial Palace.

Of the six people who were in attendance at the Emperor's request were three military leaders and three senior domestic officers. After some extended debate, the Emperor called for a vote as to whether or not the

Japanese should surrender or keep on fighting. The vote on this issue was a tie, with the three military leaders all voting to continue the war and basing their opinion on the great spiritual strength of the Japanese nation. I could not believe that anyone could vote to continue the war after the two atomic bombs had been dropped and realizing that every major city in the nation had been almost burned beyond recognition.

At this point, the Emperor took matters into his own hands and announced that this was his nation, and that he could no longer ask his people to suffer so horribly. He therefore decided Japan would sue for peace and that he would make an announcement over radio to the entire nation about this decision. After he had made a taped statement, there were still some military leaders who were trying to find the tape and destroy it. They knew that if the Japanese people heard their Emperor say that Japan was going to sue for peace, no one would object and the war would end.

After the war, I was able to go to some of the villages in Southeast Asia and work, along with medical person, with the village elders to help the civilian population. It was also vital to work with the villages, the port masters, to find out where the mines had been placed so we could get rid of them and bring in relief ships.

I ended up at Oklahoma State University, in a hurry to finish my education after five years away, taking 24 hours of credit each semester and 12 in the summer so I could earn the last 60 hours I needed within a year. I was able to take advantage of the GI Bill, the best investment this country ever made, and one that transformed the nation.

12

❧

The Occupation and Aftermath

The signing of the surrender documents aboard the *USS Missouri* took place on September 2, 1945. The previous arrangements made had been carried out to the letter, and there was no sense on the part of the American representatives that the Japanese were failing to cooperate in every respect. It was quite fitting that General Douglas MacArthur, who chaired the program, invited General Jonathan Wainwright, who was the losing commander at Corregidor and who became the highest ranking POW in the war, to accompany him when he signed the treaty. The surrender of American forces on Corregidor was a bitter pill for the United States to swallow, and the ensuing death march left a very deep impression on American servicemen regardless of to which branch they were assigned.

Following the ceremonies on the USS Missouri, the business of occupying Japan went into full force in all of its major cities. The Emperor's message to the nation about the surrender stunned everyone, and fear of the unknown as to what these hated Americans might do was on everyone's mind.

Within the first 10 days, the overall aim was to complete the disarmament of the Japanese population. Local storefronts were utilized, and both returning servicemen and civilians were required to turn in any and all weapons in their possession. Many elderly men brought in swords that had been in the family for several generations. While they offered no resistance to the order, they were decidedly sorrowful at parting with an important family heirloom. Most of the Army personnel who handled this process were quite uncaring as to the feelings of Japanese civilians.

As a nation, in 1945, Japan had been shattered by fires and bombing. Nearly every city in the nation of any size had been attacked by the American B-29s and naval carrier planes. Its merchant marine of over 12 million tons had been reduced to only 100,000 tons of coastwise shipping. The nation was short, short of medicine, short of food, short of water and short of almost everything necessary for daily living. Factories had been burned to the ground, and the landscape was barren and cluttered with ruined buildings and dumps full of destroyed items.

One of the first tasks was to get food and other essentials into Japanese seaports so that the suffering of the civilian population could be alleviated. There were two separate groups of U.S. minesweepers assigned to clearing the harbors of all underwater obstacles and any mines that had been laid during the war. This process started at Hakodate, the large naval base in the southern section of Hokkaido, where the mayor and the port commander were more than willing to cooperate. They furnished maps of where all the obstacles were located and assigned the two men who had installed the obstacles for each mine sweeper. The skippers did a great job in transferring Japanese maps to theirs in a few hours, and the work got underway. The citizens were more than happy to learn of the arrival of food and medical supplies and volunteered to unload the cargo, which had been safely packaged for shipping. Most of the ports on the coast of China and Southeast Asia had similar work done over the next few months. These efforts saved thousands of lives in Southeast Asia, bringing food and medical treatments to civilians from babies to oldsters in every nation.

Politics

The three D's of the occupation were to disarm, to demilitarize, and to deny and eliminate the characterization of the Emperor as being divine. The first two were of immediate concern and handled efficiently in a remarkably short period of time. The completion of the third "D" was fulfilled upon implementation of a revised constitution. The Meiji Constitution had been brought forth on February 11, 1889, to commemorate the creation of Japan by the Sun goddess on that same date in 660 BC. The major concern of the American occupation forces was to change the structure of the government created under the Meiji document, in which the most powerful positions in the government were held by the military.

The first postwar effort to create a new constitution involved the creation of a special constitutional committee made up of Japanese leaders to study the Meiji document and to make recommendations as to how it should be changed. This ad hoc committee consisted of approximately 30 leaders representing various political convictions. The majority of the committee had been opposed to Japanese militarism and had either spoken out or written in newspapers and other publications of their strong feelings about the military leadership of the nation. As a consequence of their actions, most of them had been put in jail for speaking out against the government. Several of them claimed to be members of the Communist Party, while others would have been considered liberals of one hue or another.

The committee set to work to review the existing constitution and make recommendations for change or to completely rewrite the document. To the utter amazement of the American administration, the committee said that it was not necessary to make any changes in the Meiji document and that rewriting the Constitution was not necessary. My only explanation for this is that the psychological force of continuity, tradition and group think in Japanese society overrode whatever liberal leanings the members of the committee may have held.

As a consequence, the American government appointed a committee of American political scientists and constitutional lawyers to create a totally new document. The document which they pieced together was approved by Japanese leaders, who had no other choice, on May 3, 1947. The role of the Emperor became one of a figurehead. The legislative branch consisted of a House of Representatives and a House of Councilors. The lower body had 411 members, with representation weighted in favor of rural areas. By the turn of the century, its membership had grown to 572. The upper house started out with 125 members, increasing over time to 252. In addition, the rules and procedures of the legislative process were changed to more closely represent the American system. The committee system, so common throughout our state and federal government, was added to the structure of the national Japanese government.

An extensive Bill of Rights was included, and procedures were introduced for reviewing the judicial processes in 10 years, with particular attention being paid to reviewing those utilized in the lower courts. The Constitution also provided that leaders of local governments were thereafter to be elected at the polls which were deemed to help strengthen local governments.

Once the Constitution was put into effect in 1952, the Japanese struggled with their interpretation of the political processes which we had put in their constitution. Eventually they worked out ways of conforming to the new document while gradually returning to their old system. In successive years thereafter, they got around many of our changes and continued doing their legislative deliberations in much the same way as before.

The concentration of power did not remain in the hands of local government; it eventually was returned to central authorities. By the year 2000, local governments were spending nearly 80% of their time filling out reports for the central government, demonstrating that they were carrying out orders from Tokyo. Labor unions, which had been allowed by the occupation government and encouraged by American labor leaders, gradually fell to the power of the major industries, tied in almost completely with various Cabinet positions in Tokyo. The last union to survive the subtle pressure was that of the National Teachers Association, which succumbed to the central government in 1989.

Of far greater importance than the mechanics of government was the creation of suffrage for women for the first time in Japanese history, as well as eliminating some of the impediments to voting for men introduced in the 1925 legislation. I might point out that, since 1952 to the present time, only one woman, Sakura Doh, has served as the Prime Minister of Japan, and that was for a short period in the 1960s. The extension of the right of women to vote in the new constitution was not an immediate change, as the number of women participating at the polls did now grow overnight.

The main political party which controlled Japan and the local governments were Liberal Democrats. The name is quite misleading, since in reality its political leanings were solidly conservative. While the leadership maintained a façade of committee functioning, along the lines with which we were in agreement, what actually transpired was that the Liberal Democratic majority functioned in many ways very similarly to the government of the prewar era. Briefly put, this meant that the political leadership of the Liberal Democrats continued to work behind the scenes in the selection of individuals for key positions in the government. This also became their way of handling political issues outside of regular committee channels and then integrating those maneuverings into a final document. The end result did not differ that greatly from our system.

Much of Japan's political success during the Occupation was because of the leadership of Shigeru Yoshida. He was a firm advocate of cooperating with the United States in almost every regard and made an excellent representative for Japan in dealing with the Occupation administration. During the first 10 years after the war ended, he was elected Prime Minister no fewer than four times. He resigned on two occasions and was shortly thereafter reelected. His influence continued whether he was in or out of office.

The other notable prime minister was Nakasone Yasuhiro, who served for five years in the 1980s. He was bitterly opposed to the postwar Occupation by the Americans and demonstrated his displeasure by always wearing black clothing in the legislature as he was mourning the status of Japan under the American thumb. He was a close friend of President Reagan and felt that the Prime Minister in Japan should be a real political leader, popularly elected, instead of chosen by party leaders.

He was so popular with the general public that the party leaders permitted him a fifth year in office rather than the traditional four-year term. He continually urged all parties to call for a new constitutional convention so that at least Japan would have a constitution written in Japanese that was really Japanese. He complained that the constitution drawn up by the Americans was not properly Japanese and that this was an insult to his nation.

Nakasone had many different ideas about how to solve existing problems, but overall he felt that a prime minister should be equal to being president of the United States and that his primary responsibility was to be a leader. He certainly behaved in this fashion in all five years that as prime minister. He continued to promote the idea of having a new convention and had generated some lively debates in the political leadership of the nation at the turn of the century, but in recent years the interest has abated. Nakasone has long since retired from political office but still speaks of the need to have a constitutional convention called to totally rewrite the existing document.

The military

The peace treaty to end the occupation of Japan was signed on September 18, 1951, and went into effect in March, 1952. At that time Japan would regain its sovereignty and function as an independent nation. Included in the documents was a security treaty between our two countries. Since the Korean War had started in 1950, it was of vital importance that Japan and the United States resolve whatever differences existed as to the final treaty of peace. While Japan would was entitled to have self-defense forces and not a regular standing army and navy, the events of the last half of the twentieth century made it imperative that the United States relax some of the restrictions included in previous negotiations in treaties with Japan. The rising threat of communism in China and North Korea caused the two nations to modify the earlier treaties in the 1980s. By the turn of the twenty-first century, Japan had the fourth or fifth largest military force in the world. The United States found no objection to this since we are now allies.

The United States was far too quick in cutting back on its military forces after the end of World War II. The lack of production of civilian goods, combined with the greater urge to bring the boys back home, created unseen difficulties at that time. We eliminated practically all production of military hardware, since we were the only nation that had not been subjected to bombing and military action in our homeland .The consequences of this were totally unforeseen.

When the North Koreans crossed the 38th parallel and invaded South Korea, the United States found itself woefully unprepared for immediate military response.

The only port available to land any American forces in South Korea was on the southern coast at Pusan. The first unit of American forces to land in Pusan was a part of the 24th Army division. I knew the battalion leader of the first group to leave Japan and go to Korea. He told me they went with a Japanese crew on an LST which had a damaged rudder, so that it could only make a 9 degree left turn. This was in stark contrast to our naval power in 1945.

The economy

One of the unforeseen consequences of the outbreak of hostilities in the Korean peninsula was its impact on the Japanese economy. During the last months of World War II, the United States Army Air Corps and Naval air forces carried out devastating raids on Japanese manufacturing establishments. Given the physical difficulties of transporting goods, both finished and raw materials inland, the Japanese had built all of their heavy industry very close to a seaport. This made it much easier to import raw materials and turn them into finished products and reship them to other countries, but it also made them easier to destroy. Admiral Marc Mitscher had neutralized every Japanese air base and facility from Tokyo to Kyushu, and continual bombing by Gen. Lemay's B-29s and B-24's on Japanese cities further contributed to the almost total annihilation of Japanese manufacturing. As a consequence, when the war came to an end the Japanese economy had a gross domestic product that was equal to only 30% of what had been its GDP in 1937. The year 1937 was chosen as a base year for economic studies and analyses of Japan since that was its last prewar year.

The destruction of Japanese shipping and manufacturing was so devastating that its recovery after the war was almost nonexistent, and there was practically no improvement during the entire period of the Occupation.

The only exception to this economic disaster for Japan was created by the outbreak of hostilities in the Korean peninsula. American participation in that conflict stimulated the demand for Japanese goods of all kinds and provided for some growth in the few months remaining before the peace treaty went into effect in the spring of 1952.

The disastrous performance of Japanese economic activity was the subject of discussions by our government, which did not want to support the Japanese for decades to come. Consequently, after the peace treaty was signed, our government extended financial aid to our former enemy. It was not at the level of the Marshall Plan for Western Europe, but it was of sufficient funds to help the Japanese recover. Not only did we extend financial assistance, but we encouraged American industry to donate unused production technology which had been developed over the last 10 years and which was vastly superior to anything that the Japanese had.

Some basic manufacturing techniques and improvements in production were extended by American industry to Japan over the next four or five years. Labor leaders in the United States invited Japanese labor leaders to come to our nation and learn about organizing workers into trade unions. This in time led to a rather extensive exchange of ideas about labor organizing and improving working conditions. These steps gradually helped Japan work its way back to being a highly productive economy.

The economy also played a role in providing more avenues for women to gain influence. The loss of life created situations where it was necessary to create job opportunities that had not previously existed. Perhaps the largest was the need to rebuild the infrastructure and manufacturing sites. Many farmers left their homes to get one of the many new jobs requiring travel of some distance. This resulted in many farms being operated by women who learned very quickly how to not only manage the physical needs of farming but also the business aspects. By the late 1950s, government studies showed that more than 750,000 women were so employed. The other major change for women has been the steady increase in those entering the political world in both their local areas and the national scene.

The decade of the 1960s proved to be a banner period for the Japanese economy. The gross domestic product (GDP) forecast by Prime Minister Eisaku Sato proved to be a most remarkable one, since Japan's GDP averaged a 13% increase each year in the 1960s. Japanese products were exported in ever increasing numbers and variety. Co-operation among several government agencies had created vital links among the industrialists, financiers, and import-export companies.

There is no exact number of government cabinet seats cast in cement in the Japanese government. Therefore, cooperation among government offices, industry, and financial interests has led to facilitating systems which are invaluable in today's international scene.

The Ministry for International Trade and Industry (MITI) can collaborate with the Bank of Japan and other cabinet officers to make it possible to expand Japanese exports. This is extremely important, since the lack of mineral resources and oil on the island constitute daily challenges to the Japanese economic planners. For Japan to have sufficient funds to buy these very necessary items, as well as raw materials that they need for, the domestic economy stipulates absolutely that the Japanese must be an exporter. The MITI organization provides constant new information to the Japanese government and the departments or agencies directly involved in the national economy.

MITI has in excess of 1400 observers in New York City watching the financial markets and the flow of goods, both raw and finished, in order to detect if there is an area in which the Japanese economy might profit. The same is true in many other countries. The ability of a relatively few Japanese who can speak Portuguese, for example, makes it possible for Japanese industry to develop overseas export markets in Portuguese-speaking nations and look for possible bargains in obtaining necessary raw materials. The role played by MITI and the Bank of Japan in sustaining and expanding the economy is in all likelihood unmatched anywhere else in the industrialized modern world.

It works like this: A refrigerator manufacturer in Sendai might be approached by MITI and asked if the company would be interested in exporting refrigerators to Brazil. The MITI representatives explains that they would loan the manufacturer sufficient funds to double his plant size and handle the trade in Brazil since he doesn't have anyone who speaks Portuguese. MITI would also guarantee him an absolute market monopoly for the northern part of Honshu where his plant was located. Given these inducements it wouldn't take too long to agree to take on this additional work. This combination of government, business, banking and foreign trade worked wonders and went a long way in explaining the success of Japan in the international business world.

13

JAPAN TODAY AND TOMORROW

In 1890, Frederick Jackson Turner, a professor at Harvard University, published an article describing the significance of the frontier in American history. In this article, the professor argues rather persuasively that American society is a relatively open society since the immediate proximity of the frontier offered anyone who had a different kind of thinking than the rest of the people in his local community could simply pack up and move west. Turner believed that the frontier provided a safety valve, not only for malcontents, but for those who wished to take the risk to strike out on their own. The sheer distances inherent on the American continent had a direct bearing on our culture.

In a similar way, Japan's geography affected the creation of its culture. Japan is approximately 140,000 square miles, smaller than several of our states. In 1850, the population of the United States was approximately 31,000,000, while in that same year, the Japanese population was also around 30 million, but crammed into a much smaller space. It is that density that explains how Japan developed.

Japanese families that came to the U.S. in the 1960s found it almost impossible to believe that we live in houses with big yards and that the woman of the household could actually get into a car and go shopping in one of our innumerable malls. They remarked frequently that it was difficult to adjust to living space in the United States after being in very compact housing units in their native land.

An executive of a very large Japanese corporation once remarked that it was company policy to keep assignments of their employees to the United States limited to not more than three years so that their transfer back to the crowded conditions in Japan would not be too difficult. Responding to surveys of high school students in several large cities, over three fourths listed going abroad for at least one time in their lifetime was a top priority.

Within the last 10 years, the birth and death rates of the Japanese population were about the same, which means that the total population numbers tend to be static. The density of population in the nation ranks it along with Belgium and other small countries in Europe. The Tokyo-Yokohama complex has a population in excess of 35 million, which is slightly more than 25% of the entire national population.

Over the past decade, there have been several movements, with government encouragement, to develop and support suburban areas or small towns within commuting distance to relieve the pressure on the major cities. This has met with partial success for the working population, but the cities are still the goal for young people who are seeking additional education or employment in metropolitan centers. There are substantial numbers of Japanese adults who have moved out of the eight largest cities into small towns or much less crowded areas and commute every day into the metropolitan center for their employment. There have been some cases reported where the commute is two hours each way. The forecast is that the concentration of the population will continue to cause problems of overcrowding for the foreseeable future.

Surveys over the last five or six years reflect that probably three out of every four Japanese adults tend to be dissatisfied with the quality of their lives. This is undoubtedly a consequence of overcrowding and a lack of recreational facilities, even though the government is trying to create more open park space in cities. The plan for increasing open areas so that people have room to enjoy themselves was experimented with in the 1960s but eventually failed due to the growing economic pressures to use these areas for business purposes.

The average life expectancy for Japanese men is now 78.6 years and nearly 85 for women, which makes the average of 81.5% as the national figure. The Japanese population is aging, and in the last 20 years, the percentage of those over 80 years of age has increased several points. In 2007, the number of those over 70 years old totaled approximately 20% of the population. Former Prime Minister Naka-sone's bright idea to purchase two Mediterranean islands as retirement homes might be rehabilitated.

Japanese society is also still largely a society of groups. From birth until at least eight or nine years of age, Japanese children are treated very permissively by their mothers who have almost exclusive responsibilities for their care. The young child basks in the home atmosphere from which they grow up with a desire to have the approval of others. This continues through their teen years during which they express themselves in a variety of ways and eventually become adults who feel that unless they belong to one or two groups they are short changing themselves.

Still another factor is that the Japanese live in a hierarchical society. Individuals are keenly aware of what level they are in and tend to respect those that are above them and probably look down on those below. The long and active role of the Japanese military establishment has certainly underscored this sense of hierarchy.

Japanese business executives each have their own council of elders, made up of former executives of the same corporation. They provide counsel to the incoming executive and have as their primary interest and concern the continuation of their corporation. They therefore act as a brake on new developments or new designs in company products.

I once watched a Japanese executive addressing a distinguished group of American executives about the future plans of his manufacturing company. Off to his right hand side in the second row of the audience were three of his council of elders. In response to questions, the new executive rather talked in general terms until he detected by nods from them that he was on the right track, at which time he talked fluently for two or three minutes.

I do not believe there will be radical design changes in products that are sold internationally by Japanese industries but only modest changes over some period of years. In a way, this keeps the wheels of industry moving with perhaps less risk that something unforeseen might happen.

The military influence

It is obvious that Japanese culture is a many-faceted thing and cannot be oversimplified when trying to explain Japanese behavior. But looking back over the last 2000 years, from the earliest settlements to the modern nation in the 21st century, it appears to me that the overriding force in Japanese culture has been that of the military. A military structure certainly emphasizes hierarchy, and the earliest records we have, the articles written in the Wei Chronicles, refer to some controlling military establishment in this primitive society. The chroniclers were unable to clearly define it, but the implications were so clear that over a period of 20 years nearly each of the chroniclers mentioned this aspect of Japanese life.

Of the six individuals who have had the greatest impact upon the development of the Japanese nation, no fewer than five of them have been military people. The great transformation from feudal Japan to that of the shogunate was the consequence of the work of Nobunaga, Hideyoshi and Tokugawa. Later, from the time the Meiji Constitution was issued in 1889 to 1922, the great debate about Japanese foreign-policy was handled by Hirobumi Ito and Yamagata Aritomo, with Yamagata the articulate spokesman for the military side of the debate.

Thus, the course of Japanese history over the last 2000 years has functioned almost always on a military agenda. The shogunate of Tokugawa and the Prussian-style Meiji Constitution both sustained the emphasis on Japanese militarism. The great justification has always been that Japan needs more areas for raw materials and mineral resources that it does not have in its homeland.

It was argued that the creation of this vast empire simply fulfills a basic economic drive and is necessity for the Japanese people. Unfortunately, the Greater East Asia Co-Prosperity Sphere never really had a chance. By the time that the Japanese had overrun all this territory, the war production achievements of the United States created the submarines and surface ships that were able to totally disrupt Japanese trade in all of these areas.

In the larger picture of all the areas overrun by Japanese forces in Southeast Asia and the heavily populated islands, this policy and the increasing difficulties Tokyo had in resupplying their forces meant that the native populations suffered extreme hardships and starvation for several years. In almost every conversation I have had with older civilians from these former Japanese-occupied areas, they reflected extreme bitterness about the practices of Japanese occupation troops.

The Japanese people knew none of the these events of how their army treated civilians, and were slow to realize exactly what had happened in prisoner of war camps as well as the exploitation of civilians in the vast areas under the control of their armed forces. The current arrangement for the Japanese military is under a joint 1980 agreement between the United States and Japan which permitted Japan to build its own defense forces as an ally of the United States. Japan's current military establishment is either the fourth or fifth largest in the world. It is my judgment that the military ventures of the past will not be repeated but that any use of Japanese military forces in the future will be in conjunction with some international body and will have as their aim the betterment of mankind.

After Japan regained its sovereignty in 1952, businessmen went abroad seeking to reestablish connections with former customers. According to the reports of these merchants and traders, they were well treated by their former associates. But a common thread running through these reestablished contacts were tales of extreme brutality on the part of Japanese occupation troops. Several accounts revealed the depth of anti-Japanese sentiment, and some businessmen were shown areas where horrifying events had taken place. Others in Japanese-occupied areas told their business friends they would be glad to see them again, except they would have to meet someplace else because it would be bad for their business if they were seen together.

Starting in 1958 and thereafter for several years, Japanese business journals and magazines carried stories written by these businessmen as to what they were learning about the conduct of Japanese occupation forces. This came as a shock to many, but the evidence was conclusive and led to some revisionist thinking in some circles of Japanese society. As an antidote to this reporting some businessmen began to write articles about some outstanding foreigners they had met while traveling overseas and with whom they had become friends. Many of these Japanese went to great lengths to ensure their new friendships would continue. Usually they would send copies of their articles to American friends and get permission to use their name in such articles.

Whether Japan would have had an option to import sufficient minerals and fuel to operate as an industrial nation in a peaceful manner has never been answered. The decision to use military force to gain what it felt it needed so desperately rather than to work through full implementation of the Open Door policy was a step in the wrong direction. The fact that it chose otherwise led to the death, suffering and starvation not only of Japan itself but in many areas of the far Pacific and the Asiatic mainland. They left scars that would probably have doomed any peacetime Greater East Asia Prosperity Sphere. The rows of white crosses all over the world give silent testimony to mankind's history.

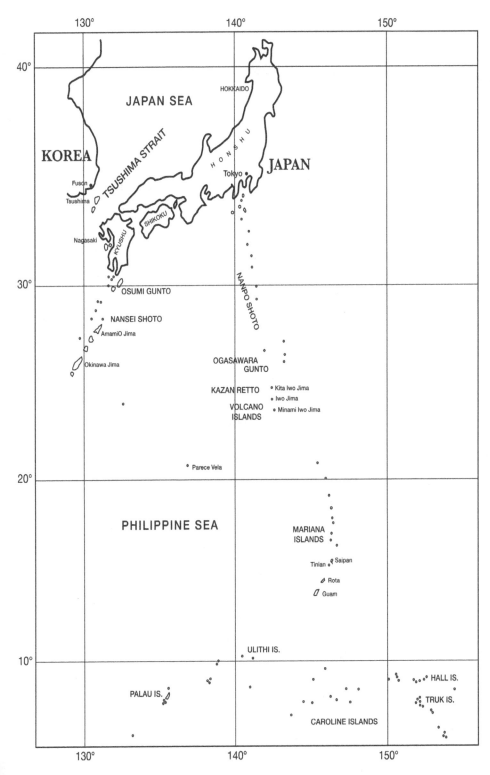

BIOGRAPHY

Noel L. Leathers was born January 14, 1924, and raised on a farm southeast of Mansfield, Ohio, in a family four boys and two girls. He moved to Columbus in 1937, graduated from Central High School and entered Ohio State University in fall of 1940.

He enlisted in the Marine Corps in spring, 1943, became a combat interpreter, and spent the next four-and-a-half years in the Pacific Theater, with landings on Tarawa, Roi-Namur and Eniwetok. Further duty took him to Japan, Korea, the coast of China and Southeast Asia.

He returned to college at Oklahoma State University in 1947 and received a bachelor's degree in 1949 and a master's degree in European history in 1950. He taught high school in Oklahoma from 1950-52 and then spent three years as a special agent in the Federal Bureau of Investigation, returning to high school teaching until 1961. In 1962, he received a Ph.D. from the University of Oklahoma in modern European history. After this, he taught history at Oklahoma State University and at the University of Toledo, where he served as a chair of the history department and eventually became dean of Arts and Sciences.

He moved to the University of Akron as academic vice president in 1972 and served as executive vice president and provost until 1972 to provost until 1985. He taught European and Japanese history until he retired in 1995, and he later returned to the school as provost from 1997 to 2000. He is the author of a book, *The Japanese in America*.

He also consulted with the government of Iran on the creation of three colleges in that country, concentrating on curriculum. He and his wife, Dr. Violet Leathers, have traveled extensively over a good part of this earth.

Made in United States
Cleveland, OH
19 May 2025

17010553R10094